PROPERTY SOLDIER

FROM THE BATTLEFIELD TO FINANCIAL FREEDOM
Overcoming Adversity and Depression to Win Big!

KEVIN PONESKIS

Contents

Introduction

My main incentive for writing this book is to raise money for a charity called Stoll, which provides accommodation, training and rehabilitation for homeless veterans. One hundred percent of the profits from the sale of this book will go to this very worthy charity. I know that some of my military friends and colleagues may choose to read this book and I ask that they resist the temptation to share it with each other without buying a copy themselves, as that won't help the charity. If someone asks to borrow it after you read it, please say this: "Sod off and buy your own you tight git," or words to that effect!

Ending up homeless is often as a result of mental illness, lack of self-worth and depression. Many veterans have suffered from the same adversity anyone can experience but add in the challenges inherent in military life such as dislocation from family and friends, long periods spent away on tours and operations and, not least, post-traumatic stress disorder as a result of these operational tours and you have the compound effect.

A Traumatic Memory

"I was told that in a couple of days I would be deploying as part of a troop to a Forward Operating base near a Place called Sangin, called Fob Robinson (Fob Rob), which is the place where Jim was killed. I must admit that it was a bit of a shock to be told this was where I would go first out of the dozens of possible places to go in Afghanistan, and I couldn't help feeling nervous because this place, more than any other place in the world spelled danger. The time to go came along soon enough and myself and about ten other guys were taken to the airstrip near the camp, where we would be taken by

Chinook helicopter (Helo) to Fob Rob. I remember looking around at the other guys who were mostly young lads in their early to mid-20s and there were some very apprehensive faces, that's for sure. I am not sure how I looked but I did my best to be as calm and reassuring as I could. As I was the most senior guy in the group, I knew it was important for me to set an example. The Chinook is a large helicopter with two rotor blades and has a ramp at the rear to allow easy access for both troops and stores. The airstrip is a very noisy and dusty place with a lot of rotor and fixed-wing aircraft coming and going at regular intervals and so I kept an eye on the tailgate of our Chinook for the signal for us all to get on.

As soon as the aircrew gave us the signal, we grabbed our heavy kit and equipment and weapons and made our way onto the back of the helicopter. The journey time was about 20 minutes long and as we set off, I was feeling a mixture of apprehension and excitement at the same time as I watched Camp Bastion grow ever smaller behind us. About ten minutes into the journey, the tail gunner approached me and shouted into my ear that our vehicle convoy, which was also en route there, was under attack as it entered Fob Rob and a firefight was currently taking place. I expected him to say that because of this we would be turning back – because a Chinook is a big 'bullet catcher' and it would be too risky to land whilst a firefight was taking place nearby – but he told me we were still going in!"…

Present Day

I am a public speaker, best-selling author and a trainer and mentor in property investment. I speak in front of hundreds of people on large stages and before going on stage, part of my prep is to take my mind to a place of confidence and self-assuredness which helps me to get 'in state' and feel strong and worthy of holding the audience's attention. The memory I shared above was a situation of feeling fearful, stressed and vulnerable; being completely out of control of what is about to happen.

This, and many other events I will share in this book, are what have shaped me into the adult I now am, both good and bad.

If you or someone you know have suffered or are suffering from any mental health challenges like I have, please know that you are not alone. There are many people feeling the same way that you do. This is not a mental health self-help book; I am not qualified to write that. I'm simply sharing my journey and experiences.

The Early Years

My journey is that of a working-class lad who joined the Royal Artillery (RA) as a 16-year-old in 1987. I served for over 24 years before leaving as a 'Regimental Sergeant Major' (RSM) in 2011. RSM is the most senior rank a soldier can achieve before that of a Commissioned Officer. As well as being a full-time soldier, for most of my Army career I was also a property investor, and when I became a civilian at the age of 40, I owned 12 houses and flats and also a 'House in Multiple Occupation' (HMO). This is a house that is let out by the room, where occupants share kitchens and bathrooms. Most people know this type of house as a student house or bedsit, although in my case I chose to rent the rooms out to working people.

After leaving the Army I carried on building the portfolio, but the significance of buying these houses during my career, and the rental income they generated, is that it allowed me to leave the Army at 40 without the need to get a job! I often repeat this statement to people when I am praising the virtues of property investing, because whilst engaged in a full-time career, it enabled me to build up rental income to a point where it could replace my job income and I could stop working for someone else. I want people to know that if I can do it, they can too. I have made plenty of mistakes along the way and it has not always been plain sailing, but the main point to make is that it's been well worth it.

Squaddie Brat

I was born in Devonport hospital in Plymouth in 1971. My mum Kathy is from Plymouth and she met and married my dad John Poneskis when he was in 29 Commando Regiment Royal Artillery based at the Royal Citadel on 'Plymouth Hoe'. The name Poneskis originated from Lithuania although the original and correct spelling is actually Poniszkis. My great grandfather emigrated to Scotland to work in the coal mines. Not long after arriving, World War One began and so he went off to fight for Britain with the Black Watch. Sadly, he was killed, however he had fathered my grandfather who also went on to work in the coal mines. When my dad Jock joined the Royal Artillery, he gave his name as Poneskis as he wanted to simplify it a little, and so it was altered from that point on.

Whilst I was growing up, Dad was posted to different Army camps around the UK and Germany. We mostly lived in Army Quarters although Mum and Dad did buy a house in Nuneaton when we were posted near there which they then rented out after we moved on. That turned out to be a bad experience for my parents as the tenants who rented the house fell into large arrears. Eventually, they were evicted and the house was sold. Although my dad's first experience as a landlord was not a good one, after he left the Army he became a full-time property investor himself and did very well. I am glad he didn't allow his bad experience to put him off as it was my dad who first encouraged me to invest in property in my early 20s.

Like the number of houses we lived in, it's just as hard to work out how many different schools I went to growing up. It was hard to make long-lasting friendships and obviously academically it was impossible to stick to a normal curriculum as each time we moved schools, the new school would either be ahead of the previous school or behind, and sometimes we would even be learning a subject that the previous school wasn't even teaching. Mum and Dad recognised that our schooling was suffering and so they decided that their three older kids – me, Debbie and Johnny – should go to boarding school in order to get some educational stability. I was nine years old at the time but relatively confident and self-assured for my age. My younger sister Lisa was only seven and the 'baby of the family' and so it was decided that Lisa should stay at home at least for the time being.

Due to the impact service life has on kids' education, you will find a relatively high percentage of kids at boarding school are 'forces' kids, or 'squaddie brats' in the case of an Army parent. Boarding school fees can be very expensive especially for multiple children from the same family and so the Armed Forces provide financial support to servicemen and women to enable them to send their kids to boarding school in order to provide some stability and continuity. Boarding school allowance (as it was known at the time) was capped at a certain level for each child, which meant that if a parent wanted to send their kids to a better school, they would have to pay out of their own pocket to enable that. Army wages are not the highest and my dad also provided some financial support to his older children Marion and Tommy, still living with their mum in Scotland; so, as my parents couldn't afford to add much to the allowance provided, they had to choose from a list of schools that were within their budget.

The Beatings

"I'm in the classroom with all the other kids and there isn't a teacher here. We are all talking and laughing with each other and the volume is really loud. I can't find my crayons for the next lesson ... oh wait ... the boy next to me has them! "You've taken my crayons you punk!" Everything has suddenly gone quiet. The headmaster is standing in the doorway and has heard my bad language! He is furious and his eyes are focussed directly on me. The panic and fear I

am feeling is intense. He comes towards me like he is about to engage in mortal combat, pushing aside chairs and desks that are in his path with such ease it is as if they weigh nothing at all. He reaches me, sitting frozen with fear, and grabs my hair with one hand and with brute force drags me out of the room by the hair like a rag doll. I bounce off chairs and desks on my way out of the classroom, but the biggest collision I feel is against the doorframe. I am holding on to his hands to take some of my own weight from my hair, but I lose my grip as he twists his hand and the pain returns to my scalp. We are at his office now and he has let go of my hair. "Bend over with your hands on the table," he says. I'm terrified, so I do as I'm told and try not to cry. The caning is really painful and I put my hands in the way of the cane to protect myself, but that's making the headmaster angry and he's getting more forceful. Now at last he feels he has administered the appropriate amount of pain to fit my crime and stops hitting, leaving me with broken skin."

I was quite a wilful child and would often be referred to as the class joker. One headmaster and I did not see eye to eye and he seemed very keen to knock this naughtiness, as he saw it, out of me. Corporal punishment was perfectly legal at the time and his method of administering this form of punishment was with a cane. At least it was in my case. I am afraid that there was a certain level of extra cruelty involved with his punishment as he would often make the unfortunate child wait outside of his office for some time to be caned, and for those kids who knew what was coming it was not a happy time waiting. In fact, the wait was sometimes worse than the cane itself. However, if the punishment deemed necessary was severe then the caning would be harsh in terms of repetition and force used. I often wonder after his temper subsided on these occasions if he ever felt shame or remorse, but I suppose I will never know. On one occasion, my sister Debbie and a concerned teacher took me to the local GP for treatment for the welts on my backside as they weren't healing sufficiently and had got infected. I am sure if a child of nine years was presented to a doctor today with the same injuries the police would immediately be called and action taken against the adult responsible, but as we know the law as well as attitudes were different then and so nothing was done by the authorities to intervene.

A few years ago, I attended a school reunion with Debbie and Johnny and we heard from an older pupil about when he had his front tooth knocked out by the same headmaster with his fist. He also remembered an incident when the headmaster grabbed me by the hair during dinner and banged my head repeatedly on the table. Johnny who would only have been about 11 himself, tried to defend me but was pushed away.

The Fun Part

Having my older siblings Debbie and Johnny at the same school was comforting. I excelled at running and I was the second-best runner at the school at the time. The best runner was a 15 or 16 years old and I was 9 or 10 during my time there. I remember during a distance race that another older pupil asked me not to beat him as he could tell I was strong, but I tried my very best to win the race, especially as my dad was there to watch. I ended up coming a worthy second to the best runner with the other pupil coming third. I remember being worried that he might beat me up afterwards for embarrassing him, but I am pleased to say he didn't, because he was clearly not a bully, which as far as I am concerned makes him a much bigger person than simply being good at running.

The Great Escape

Even though I enjoyed being at the school overall, I was getting more and more unhappy with the headmaster's behaviour, because it just seemed so unjust and unfair to me. I was frustrated and angry because I knew something was wrong, but I didn't really know what to do about it. My dilemma was that I didn't actually want to leave the school. My parents had asked me if I wanted to leave as they were aware that I was being quite harshly treated, but they didn't know the full extent. I remember telling them that I didn't want to leave and that everything would be ok, because I would stop being naughty and stay out of his way and stay out of trouble. They knew that I was capable of being quite naughty and unruly and so – bearing in mind that the cane and the slipper in schools was perfectly normal at the time – it must have been difficult for them to know what to do for the best. Things eventually came to a head when I decided to run away from the school in order to rebel. I knew that the punishment for this would be very severe, but I was prepared to face the consequences anyway. I convinced another pupil whose name I can't remember (if you ever read this book please get in touch) to run away with me and off we both went into the countryside. The other lad wasn't as committed as me to staying on the run and before nightfall he decided to head back to school to face the music. I slept rough in a barn which had hay in it and thankfully it wasn't too cold. I had some food stolen from the kitchen, so I didn't get too hungry on the first day. I was still intent on staying out, although the food had now gone and I was feeling a bit dishevelled. Luckily, I befriended a lad of a similar age who lived on the nearby farm that the barn belonged to, and he brought me some food. The farmer's son thought it was extremely exciting to be harbouring a fugitive boarding school runaway and was willing to help as long as I didn't dob him in!

My resolve had wavered by the next day and I found myself walking back in the direction of the school. As you would expect, the police were out looking for me and sure enough a police car pulled up on the country lane I was on and I didn't run, but accepted being captured – or was it rescued? That was an uncomfortable trip back to the boarding house, because what on earth was the headmaster going to do this time, and how much was it going to hurt?

After being returned to the school it was actually a very surreal time. I wasn't beaten, because he had obviously come to the conclusion that it had gone past that with me. Instead, he decided to expel me from the school with immediate effect. I was made to sit alone in a room for hours and made to write pages and pages of lines saying, "I must not run away from school I must not run away from school" and so on. Meanwhile my parents had been told that I was to leave the school immediately, so they asked my Uncle Eddy and his wife Karen (who lived much closer than them) to come and collect me and my things from school, and that was the end of my time there. My sister and brother stayed on at the school for a while, although when Mum and Dad learnt the full truth about my treatment, they set about removing Debbie and Johnny as well. Debbie was a school prefect and didn't get into much trouble – and in any case the girls only got the slipper not the cane. Johnny did get the cane from time to time but not as badly as I did. The reason Debbie and Johnny couldn't be removed immediately was the Army rules dictated that if a parent removed a child or children from boarding school without giving enough prior notice, then the Army could claim thousands of pounds of fees back from the parent. Once Mum and Dad went through the proper channels and proved to the

Army that I had been mistreated at the school, the Army allowed Debbie and Johnny to be removed early. I know my mum and dad argued with each other about this, but my dad's commanding officer repeatedly warned him not to remove them early because of the possible financial consequences that my parents definitely could not afford. The other boy who ran away with me was only suspended as it was established that I was the ringleader. To this day I don't know if deep down I knew that by running away and causing so much fuss I would inevitably have to leave the school, but ultimately it caused me and the headmaster to part company which was clearly in my best interest.

My view of corporal punishment in schools is mixed due to my own experience. I am sure that if I had never met that headmaster, or any other overzealous teacher who went too far when administering corporal punishment, it is likely that I might have said things like "didn't do me any harm" and "kids today need a bit more discipline." But what my time at the that school taught me is that if it is legal to hit children, then you are exposing all children to those teachers who are capable of being too violent and too cruel and who can cause lifelong issues. Some of the programmes that are on TV today show that there are much better techniques that can and should be used by both parents and teachers alike to discourage bad behaviour in kids without the need for violence. I know it's very difficult for teachers though, and I do not envy them at all when trying to control unruly children in the classroom who can often be violent themselves towards the teachers. I have less sympathy for parents who are too physical when administering discipline to their kids though, and I remember a sketch by the comedian Billy Connelly when he mimicked a parent whacking a child for whacking his younger brother, whilst saying, "How many times have I told you that it's wrong to hit people smaller than you?" Clearly the point is, if we hit kids to make them conform then what are we teaching them? I think that it takes a lot more skill and ultimately more work as a parent to discipline without hitting. As an adult, I have not always felt this way on the subject because my views have altered as I have aged and been exposed to alternative methods. I remember smacking my daughter Siân when she was a toddler, but after one such incident I suddenly felt ashamed and something changed in my head which caused me to never do it again. If you disagree with me on this it is clearly your prerogative, but if I ever saw an adult hitting a child and I thought for one second that it was excessive, I wouldn't hesitate to intervene. I actually became much angrier about that headmaster's treatment of me as a child when I grew older, because it was only then that I realised just how wrong it had been.

Fresh Start

After being expelled, I went to a local school in Plymouth before going to a different boarding school. I was happy to attend boarding school again, because it really suited my independent nature. I have always been a very independent person with a strong sense of adventure, and boarding school for me was exciting. I know the picture I painted earlier of my time at the first boarding school wasn't a good one, but experiences like that are rare. The next school was a much larger and more modern school with much better facilities. The school had a separate boarding house and accommodation blocks near to the main school which was state-run. There was a strong sporting ethos which I liked a lot. I played a lot of sport, but what I was best at was running. At this time, my dad was training for the New York Marathon and during the school holidays my brother and I would go out and run with him, sometimes as much as 13 miles. For a lad that was already naturally good at running, this extra training made me extremely fit indeed which helped me win the school cross country by a huge margin. The teachers, unaware of all the extra training I had been doing, thought I might be an athletic star of the future – which clearly didn't happen, but it was nice to get such a lot of positive recognition at the time.

Daddy's Boy

As often happens with boys at school, the ones who excel physically are often given more respect by the other kids, and so I benefitted from this (or so I thought). As we know, intellect and wisdom are much more impressive attributes as we grow older, but not so for 11-year-olds. As we know, kids also associate importance and standing with that of their fathers, and to boys of that age my dad was an impressive man. He had risen through the ranks in the Army (starting at private) and reached captain. He had been in the Special Air Service (SAS) and also an Army Commando Regiment. He had excelled in boxing and football, representing the Army (not a sub unit or regiment but the whole of the British Army) in both, and later went on to coach Army standard boxers and footballers. On his way to becoming a Captain, he was the RSM of Woolwich when it was the Adult Training Regiment for The Royal Artillery. In hindsight, I think I was too boastful about my father to the other boys. In the boarding house, there were about 12 boys in my age group and we shared a dormitory. At least for the first year I seemed to be the alpha male of this group. Looking back, I know that I got far too big for my boots with the others and this caused resentment towards me. There wasn't a scouts' group or Army cadet force for us to join, so we collectively decided (Or did I? I can't remember!) to form our own version of cadets, and I was placed in charge. I would march the others around and lead them in mock battles in the nearby woods. I can't remember exactly what caused what followed, but as a group all the other boys (of my age) in the boarding house collectively made a decision to oust me as the leader and to stop speaking or associating with me altogether! This continued for many weeks and things didn't ever return to normal. A boarding school can be a very lonely place indeed if no one speaks to you. I can remember feeling utterly ashamed and embarrassed that I would have to sit alone in the dining hall, with everyone pointing and whispering about it. I know that this time in my life knocked my self-confidence and my self-esteem a lot. It made me terrified of being ostracised by 'the group', and it caused me problems right into my adult years because, due to this fear I would try too hard to be liked, and others could see this weakness and fear in me which actually compounded the problem. It also gave me a fear of being in charge or in a position of authority over others. This fear caused me huge problems in my early years in the Army that's for sure! Things did eventually go back to a sort of normality and other boarders in my year did start to speak to me again, although I didn't ever relax around the main ring leaders who had controlled the others against me for what seemed like an eternity. I knew then that I would never want to put myself in that position again, because from the head position you can be dragged back down to earth with a bump – and the bottom rung of a ladder is a lonely place to be! I know that kids turning on other kids is very common in all schools and most people will have experienced it at some time growing up. I suppose the fact is that if it happens in a boarding school there is very little respite or escape. I did need to be taken down a peg or two, but the isolation I suffered took me down too far and I am convinced that as well as my treatment at the hands of my old headmaster, the combined effect had a long-lasting impact on my self-confidence and self-esteem until my late 20s. Of course, these inner feelings can be masked to others to a certain degree, but feelings inside are very debilitating and make life a constant struggle in both relationships and work alike.

The Entrepreneur Dad

At the time my dad left the Army, he was being told by his superiors that he could have climbed as high as a Quarter Master Lieutenant Colonel. But he chose to take a chance on making a success of himself in Civvy Street instead. His good friend Tommo, who he had served with in 22 SAS and 29 Commando (Cdo) Regt., invited my dad to join him in running (as lease owners) Barking Football Social Club in Essex. It was quite a gamble to take for my dad because a long-term career in the Army does provide relative stability financially with a pension to look forward to. So it is a big step to turn your back on it. As we all know becoming a business owner is fraught with financial risk. Indeed most fail – especially in a business where the person has relatively little experience. My dad's superiors tried hard to convince him not to go, but he held firm, which I am pleased to say for him was the right decision, as he and Tommo made it a success and made some good money. When Dad left the Army, it was decided that the family home would be in Plymouth and so he shared a house with Tommo in Essex. Sadly, the separation put too much strain on the marriage and my mum and dad got divorced when I was 14. The main impact this had on me was living with the effect it had on my mum and trying to stoically absorb her grief and console her. I have painful memories of this time which I struggled with as a child.

Soldier or Property Entrepreneur?

Junior Leaders

It was now the summer of 1987 and I had at this stage already decided to join the Army. I knew that school wasn't for me as it had proved to be too stressful and so any further education at this point wasn't something I was in favour of. My dad had been in the Royal Artillery and so that is where I wanted to go. If a boy joined the Artillery at 16, he would go to a Junior Leaders Regiment Royal Artillery in Bramcote Camp near Nuneaton, and spend a year there being trained before joining an Adult Regiment in either the UK or Germany. On three separate occasions during my childhood, Dad had been posted to Bramcote Camp, so I knew it was going to be a very familiar place to go. Before actually joining the Army, I met another 16-year-old called Gary at the Army Careers recruitment office in Plymouth. Gary was also from Plymouth and as we were both joining the Royal Artillery, we knew we would be travelling back and forth together on leave. We got on straight away and after signing for the 'Queen's Shilling' (which meant you were committed to joining up), which was about a fiver at the time, we both went to a nearby café where we bought big Cornish pasties as a treat.

The next time Gary and I met was at Plymouth train station on 27th October 1987 which was the day we were to report to Bramcote Camp. My mum dropped me off and I said goodbye outside before making my way with my bags to the platform. I felt pretty calm and collected because it didn't feel like I was stepping into the unknown, as it must do for most lads leaving home at 16 and joining the Army. A lad called Brads who also 'joined up' that day was waiting on the platform as well. Brads and I would end up in 'Mansergh' troop, whereas Gary joined Nicholson troop which was downstairs in the same building. I have often ribbed Gary about the fact that he had a lot of his family to see him off on the platform, and after saying all his goodbyes he joined us on the train still a little bit tearful. On arrival at Nuneaton train station, we were met by some NCOs from the camp and marshalled onto the waiting minibuses and taken to Bramcote Camp.

My first Troop photo – front row furthest right

Things started to happen a lot quicker now and all of the Army instructors seemed to be shouting all of the time! Throughout my Army Career, I was made very aware of the impact my dad had on people during his career. He was very well-respected and also feared by most, as he was known as a hard and stern man, and my first day in the Army would make me acutely aware of this legacy. Each troop would have two Sergeants in charge of it as well as a Troop Commander, who would either be a young officer or a Sergeant

Major. Sergeants would do two years as an instructor at Bramcote; one would be starting his first year there and the other would be starting his second year, and he would be the 'Troop number one'. My troop was Mansergh troop which was named after a famous General. The other troops were also named after famous Generals who had previously served in the British Army. My troop number one was a Scotsman called Sergeant Hogg who was calling out the nominal roll for the very first time. When he called out my name, he stopped and looked up from his sheet of paper. He said, "Which one of you is Poneskis?"

I raised my hand a little nervously.

"Are you related to Jock Poneskis?"

"Yes Sergeant, he is my dad."

He stared at me and then said, "Your old man is Jock Poneskis?"

"Yes Sergeant."

The whole room was silent; everyone was looking at me and there was tension in the air. Sergeant Hogg just stared at me for what seemed like ages. He then said, "Poneskis, your old man used to give me fuck all, so I am going to give you fuck all!" I was told to immediately start doing press-ups. The irony is that my dad used to get me and my brother to do lots of press-ups as kids and would often show off to his mates by saying, "Kevin, show us how many press-ups you can do" – which was usually about 50 proper ones, which I was very proud of, so I think Sgt Hogg would have been impressed at how many press-ups I could do on my first day. Sergeant Hogg treated me very fairly throughout my year at Bramcote. It turned out that he had and still does have a lot of respect for my dad and he was only pulling my leg at the time about how much I was going to have to pay for what my dad had put him through – luckily for me!

The next thing to be done was for all of us to go and have our first military haircut – and yes, it is like you see in the movies where a line of long-haired lads is queuing to go into the barbers, and other lads are walking out the other end rubbing their grade 2 shaved heads because it feels so weird.

Unfortunately, I looked even weirder than most because I have a long semi-circular scar on my head that is visible when I've got a shaved head. I got it on my fifth birthday in Germany when out playing with my brother and sister whilst my mum was getting everything ready at home for my birthday party. I thought it would be a good idea at the time to crawl under a fast-moving roundabout in the playground, the flooring of which was covered with sand. To stop the sand clogging up the roundabout there was a metal girder attached to the underside. I am sure the designer didn't imagine that this sharp length of metal would also serve to prevent a child's head from fouling the roundabout as well! I can still remember looking up after crawling underneath and seeing the metal girder coming towards me before everything went dark. My brother and sister helped pull me out by my feet and I regained consciousness. The top skin of my head had been taken off. Luckily, a few inches of my scalp were still intact and stopped my scalp from falling to the floor. I started to run in the direction of the Army medical centre which isn't the best thing to do to restrict bleeding, and I was bleeding a lot! The other kids were running after me but none of them could catch me as I was running that fast. Luckily for me, a soldier saw me running and covered in blood and he did catch up with me. He scooped me up and then continued to run himself in the direction of the medical centre so I could get some urgent treatment. Meanwhile, Debbie and Johnny ran home and told my mum that they thought Kevin might be dead!

It must have been an awful shock for my mum to run to the medical centre as a German civilian ambulance arrived to rush me to hospital not knowing if I was alive or dead.

I did however have a lucky escape and, after spending many weeks in a German hospital, I was left with a very large scar on my head which is mostly hidden as long as my hair isn't too short! After getting my new Army haircut the other lads thought it was hilarious that Poneskis now looked like a tennis ball with big ears, and I had to agree with them.

As a new recruit you either have to run or march everywhere. The days are very long: starting at 6am, with lights out at 10pm. There would be lots of physical training as well as classroom-based learning as well. We would be woken every morning to the song *You're in the Army Now* by Status Quo, which was played at a really high volume and repeated over and over which was a bit surreal. It was like being subjected to some kind of mental conditioning that a prisoner of war might expect. You basically started rushing around from the minute you were woken, and after having a shower and shave and cleaning your teeth you would do 'block jobs' which was basically cleaning, sweeping and polishing the accommodation. After this was done, you would 'fall in' outside in three ranks before being marched to the 'cook house' for breakfast. All mealtimes in the early months were stressful occasions because you were always really hungry but were hardly given enough time to actually eat. The instructor would decide which rank (of the 3) would go in first, then second, then third. Being in the first rank to enter or even second would buy you valuable eating time inside and so it was a 3x daily wish to not be last in. After what seemed like seconds sat down with your food, the instructor would shout for his troop to get outside which you had to do whether you had only just started eating or not.

You would often be wolfing down food whilst queuing to empty your plate into the swill bin whilst being shouted at to "Fucking hurry up and get outside." The whole regime of putting new recruits under pressure is designed to weed out those who find it too hard to cope mentally and physically. If my memory serves me correctly about half of those who start basic training either leave voluntarily or are told they are not up to scratch and also leave as a result. There was no way I was going to quit and I can remember being really afraid of getting into any trouble and being told to leave.

My insecurity and fear of rejection caused me problems at this point because again I tried too hard to make the other lads like me. I would tell jokes after lights out but instead of getting laughs the lads just took me as being a bit weird as the jokes probably weren't that funny, as I obviously wasn't at ease. I didn't really forge a strong friendship with anyone in my troop but Gary remained my friend.

One of my block jobs was brushing and mopping and polishing the stairs every morning. Gary's troop (Nicholson) was on the ground floor of the building, and we would say hello during block jobs as he would be cleaning and polishing the downstairs corridor. Our usual brief conversation would often revolve around how long it was till we would be back in Plymouth for Christmas leave and a few beers. It's at this point that the full year ahead seems like an eternity, but it does indeed pass, and the 'Pass Off' parade is the last day as a Junior Soldier. Everyone's family is invited to watch their boys march around the square in full dress uniform accompanied by the Royal Artillery's military band, as well as other military displays that are laid on to entertain the families. It's a special day for the lads who have made it through and have now officially been accepted into the British Army, and also the proud families who one year before had waved off a 16-year-old boy and are now seeing a proud young man who has grown up a great deal. One disappointment I had that day was not wearing any rank on my arm to show my family – especially my dad! During the year at Bramcote, the junior soldiers who are deemed good enough are promoted and given the rank of Junior Lance Bombardier (one stripe), Junior Bombardier (two stripes) and Junior Sergeant (three stripes). In a troop of about 25 passing out, there would be one Junior Sergeant, two Junior Bombardiers and four to six Junior Lance Bombardiers. Statistically, those who are awarded rank whilst at Junior Leaders usually go on to do well in the Army. Gary was proudly wearing two stripes and he went on to earn the rank of Sergeant Major during his Army Career. I am pleased to say that I did manage to buck the trend having not achieved any rank whilst in training, as I earned the rank of Regimental Sergeant Major during my career before I retired in 2011 which, including my time as a 'boy soldier', was over 24 years in the Army.

One thing I found fascinating was seeing my dad and Sergeant Hogg meet again after so many years. Dad, who was now doing well with the football club, pulled up outside of my block in his big posh car pretending that he wasn't too sure where he was supposed to park it. Throughout my dad's time in the Army, he only ever had an old banger of a car and I bet a young Gunner Hogg was one of the soldiers my dad would get to push him along to try and 'bump start' it. Dad got out of the car and I re-introduced him to Sgt Hogg, who my dad remembered well as dad was his boxing and football coach. It was quite strange to see Sgt Hogg take on a totally different persona to the bullish and quite scary person I had become used to, in that he was now very quiet and respectful and hung off my dad's every word! It must have been a nice feeling for my dad to show that in addition to doing well in the Army, he was now doing well for himself in Civvy Street as well.

Prior to the passing out parade, Gary and I learnt that we would both be posted to the same regiment which was 14 Field Regiment based at Larkhill near Salisbury. Larkhill is right on the edge of Salisbury Plain which is where most of the artillery exercises and live firing takes place. We were not in the same Battery (Regimental sub-unit), as I was in 34 Bty and Gary was in 76 Bty, but we still regularly went down to the town drinking together and would always travel back to Plymouth together at weekends and on leave, where we would both drive around in our first ever cars. I had an old Datsun 120Y and Gary had an old mini-van with Union flags on the side.

The 29 Commando Dream

I initially went to 14 Regiment but my ambition was always to get into 29 Commando (Cdo) Regiment (Regt) Royal Artillery (RA) and earn the coveted Green Beret. 29 Cdo is based mainly in Plymouth (there are sub-units of it in Poole and Arbroath which I will come to later) and is also where my dad was serving when he met my mother. Gary also wanted to go there at some point, but not yet. To get into the Commando Regiment you have to pass a very arduous course split into two parts. The first part is called the Pre-Commando Course (cse) or 'beat up' which is three weeks long and run by 29 Cdo in Plymouth. The second part is the 'All Arms Commando Course' (AACC) which is eight weeks long and run by the Royal Marines. As it is a very demanding course to pass physically, Gary and I decided to wait till we were a bit stronger before attempting it. After all, we were still only 17! I was now over 6ft tall, but only 10.5 stone in weight, so I definitely had some filling out to do. The other influence on my decision not to go sooner rather than later was my dad, who said I should wait until I reached the rank of Sergeant before trying for 29 Cdo. His theory was that you could reach the rank of Sergeant quicker in the regular Field Army, so I should wait till then and be physically stronger, probably in my early to mid-20s, and still be on track to reach WO1 and maybe further by the end of my 22-year (normal career span) adult service.

Gary and I were not in sync to go for it at the same time which probably would have made it easier for us if we could have trained together and supported each other through it as close mates do. The Artillery also has a Parachute Regiment called 7 Para Royal Horse Artillery (7 Para RHA) and to get into that you have to volunteer and do a pre course followed by 'P Company' with the Paras, and if you are successful you are awarded the coveted Maroon Beret and can then go on to attend the Military Parachute Course and be allowed to wear Parachute wings. A few years later, Gary went to Plymouth to try the course before I did. But a combination of things, one of them lower leg injuries, prevented him from passing.

Chasing Promotion

As I mentioned earlier Larkhill is where most of the Artillery go. After a couple of years, I was selected to attend my first leadership course which qualifies you for promotion from Gunner (Gnr) to Lance Bombardier (LBdr). It was a 14 Regt leadership course and Gary was also on it. As he had already displayed in basic training, he had good leadership skills and he was awarded top student and immediately promoted to Lance Bombardier (LBdr). I was pleased for him but also a little envious as well. At the pass-off parade, in front of his proud family, Gary was presented with a drill cane with a plaque on it that stated that he came top of the leadership course, and it still has pride of place in his house today – and rightly so. My mum was there and had to look on at me as one of the 'also rans' again. My lack of self-confidence meant I was nowhere near competing with Gary for top student at the time. I can remember that I was really relieved not to be awarded the 'most improved student' award which in most cases means you started pretty bad and ended up average. I did however get promoted as well a few months later, so at the age of 20 I was doing ok and this helped a little with my self-confidence as at last my value as a soldier and a person had been noticed.

Tug of War

One way of doing something other than go out on to the ranges every day at Larkhill, was playing and representing the Regt at sport. If it was a sport with regimental backing, you could be put into full-time training for many weeks leading up to big competitions and spend your days in sports gear and not going out on to ranges every day. Gary had already gotten involved in the regimental Tug of War team and he convinced me to give it a go as well. Tug of War is a very hard sport indeed because there is nowhere to hide on a rope! If your legs and arms have gone and you literally cannot hold on to the rope any more, you are in a very uncomfortable place – and it was a place I found myself in more often than I'd like to admit. Most people's perception of a Tug of War competition is when the biggest and fattest blokes bounce out of a pub, and after a bit of a heave ho, return to the pub and get even bigger and fatter!

Competitive Tug of War is somewhat different because each team pulls in a particular weight category. Eight men will pull in each category and these eight men will stand on large eight-man scales and all together will need to be on or below the weight for that category. The main weight categories in competitions are 560 kg, 600 kg, 640 kg and 680 kg. The average man's weight respectively is 70 kg (11 st) 75 kg (11.8 st) 80 kg (12.6 St) and 85 kg (13.4 st). So, a bit like in boxing you actually need to shed as much excess weight as possible to get into the lower weight category to give yourself the best chance against your opponent. What tends to happen is that the coach is constantly trying to get the strongest eight guys into a category and will inevitably ask each guy to lose a certain amount of weight to get those eight into the category below what their current weight is. I ended up losing a lot of weight and by the end of my second season at nearly 6ft 2 I weighed only 11 stone! The training for Tug of War is very tough – at least it is if you want to win competitions. Our coach Mike, whose nickname was (and still is) Beano was a hard taskmaster when it came to training because he really wanted us to go on to become Army champions. We came close in 1992, our first year, and we managed to win the 640 kg category the following year. We then went on to represent the Army against the RAF and the Navy and won that competition also. It was a very proud moment for the team, but especially so for Beano who had been involved in Tug of War his whole Army career, and he was now close to retiring. As with any tough sport the coach is in a difficult position in that he has to push the guys pretty hard and this does cause a lot of tension and arguments. I can remember lots of rows and even a punch up at Earls Court which was a competition called the 'Royal Tournament' which sadly isn't on any more but was a fantastic event with lots of things for the many thousands of spectators to enjoy –such as the Naval Field Gun Competition, The King's Troop Royal Horse Artillery display, motorbike display teams to name but a few, and also military Tug of War. Beano had put a curfew in place and said we were only allowed two beers the night before as we were in competition the next day. There were a few rebellious guys in our team and Beano entered the bar at curfew time and ordered us all to get to bed. A couple of the lads didn't like being pushed in the direction of the door and before I knew it a punch-up had started with Beano, who was a fair bit bigger that anyone else, in the middle of it! The fight was soon broken up and we all went to bed, but a fight or a row always seemed to be simmering just beneath the surface in our team. After the competition was over, in which we reached the semi-finals, we were allowed to drink – and let me just say that some of the guys in our team liked to drink a lot, so trouble was never far away! The next morning most of us were pretty hung over and some probably still drunk. We were waiting on our bus for Beano to hand back our accommodation that we had been using at Earls Court. A few of the lads noticed that there was an Army flatbed truck next to our bus which had some really nice furniture on it that would look nice in our accommodation back at camp. Nicking from an individual is a 'no-no', but for squaddies if it belongs to the military it's fair game, and if it isn't nailed down and it's 'shiny' it's as good as gone. Onto our bus went lamps and chairs and small tables and anything else that would come in handy. Beano later got on the bus and noticing we were all a bit quiet asked what we had been up to, to which we all replied "nothing". He squinted his eyes at us and took his seat, obviously unconvinced, but deciding to let it go. Just before the bus could leave the arena, we were stopped by a load of military police who seemed to be a little too excited about the fact that we'd nicked some furniture. We soon learnt that hard drugs had been hidden in and around the furniture, and in the next display the public were about to see how clever the Army's sniffer dogs were at finding these drugs. Needless to say, we were all in the shit, and unfortunately more so for Beano as he was supposed to be in charge of this drunken, brawling, drug-laced furniture stealing rabble! As soon as we got back to Larkhill, we all had to get into service dress and report to the Commanding Officer and the RSM for a good bollocking. Luckily, apart from extra guard duties that's as far as the punishment went, although moments like these were certainly not good for career progression.

Although there was quite a big difference in our age, I got on pretty well with Beano and I liked his sense of humour. About 15 years later as a Sergeant Major, I happened to be back at Larkhill and I could hear the distinctive noise of a Tug of War competition and so I wandered over to take a look for old time's sake. The two teams were giving their all and in between them, judging it, was Beano. When I was able to, I went over to say hi. His wife Wendy was there and his kids, Vicky and Robert, who had only been about ten when I knew them; they both really surprised me as without any prompting both said, "Hello Pony." We all had a really good chat and we promised to keep in touch and visit each other which I am pleased to say we do regularly, when we normally enjoy a round of golf which usually costs me money in lost bets, and we always enjoy copious bottles of red wine.

Following Dad into Property

In 1991, I bought my first ever property so that was a significant year for me. By this time, my dad was doing well investing in property and so he encouraged me to do the same. My mother was selling her flat in Plymouth and we decided that it would be good to get myself 'on the property ladder'. I was still living in Larkhill and so I rented the flat out which covered the mortgage. I have still got this flat today as it works well as a rental. When it comes to which properties work best as rental income generators and which don't, it always comes down to tenant demand. By that, I mean how many people are looking for the type of property you have in that part of town, at that rental amount.

It just so happened that my mum's old flat ticked all the right boxes as the rent is and was affordable to most, in that it sits slightly above what the local authority will pay out in housing benefit to the right applicant. I use the term the 'right applicant' because certain people are entitled to more housing benefit than others, which is usually down to their age.

It's very near a bus route, is close to the shops, and is also a relatively short walk into town. The flat isn't in the best part of town, but it isn't in the worst, either.

A rule of thumb when selecting a good area to buy a rental property is: don't buy it in a really rough area because you can get it cheap, but just outside of the rough area is fine. If you can find a patch like this that has a good number of owner-occupiers as well as people renting there, you will be ok.

The biggest mistake people make with property investing is they buy a house to rent out that they would like to live in themselves. A typical example of this is a three-bed semi in a nice suburb. The problem with this type of house is tenant demand and gross yield. Let's say the rent for this house is £650 per calendar month. There will be 5 times more people looking to find a £500 per calendar month (pcm) place which ticks all of the boxes that I mentioned earlier. So, what happens is greater void periods in between tenants, which can be very expensive, especially if you decide to spend money on the place upgrading it during this void. When I mentioned gross yield, this is the annual rent the property can achieve divided by the purchase price multiplied by 100 (to make it a percentage). Using Plymouth as an example, I know that my flat is currently worth about £75K and it rents out with hardly any voids for £500 pcm. I have had a quick look at Rightmove and just down the road in a suburb of Plymouth, called Plymstock, you can pick up a 3-bed semi for about £150K which will rent out at for approximately £650 pcm. So, the gross yields are as follows:

Flat in Cattedown: £500 x 12 / £75000 x 100 = 8%
House in Plymstock: £650 x 12 / £150000 x 100 = 5.2%

Therefore, to only get £150 pcm more in rent you have to pay twice as much for the property, but if you had a one-month void more than the flat per year, you've wiped out £650 of this extra rent, and the voids could easily be a lot longer. It is also worth remembering that the landlord has to pay the bills for the house during void periods as well. This may or may not include council tax depending on the rules for empty properties at the time. A much smarter thing to do would be to buy two flats for £75K, instead of the one house, which would give you the following with less voids!

Flat annual rent: £6000 x 2 = £12000
House annual rent: £7800

What many untrained landlords do is rent out their old house if they don't have to sell it after they move, because they think this is a wise thing to do financially. In most cases this isn't the wisest thing to do – unless your old place is a terraced house or flat in a cheap part of town. I was pretty lucky to get good advice at the time to buy my mum's old flat and to rent it out. I was able to get a 100% mortgage then and even with high interest rates at the time (14 %), the rent has always covered the mortgage since 1991. I wish I had gone out and bought many more of this type of flats or houses in Plymouth at the time, but hindsight is a wonderful thing! It was a few years later before I bought another property, but in the meantime, I had bought a good asset that is still serving me well today.

Becoming a Father Myself

Around the time I got involved in Tug of War, I also met a girl who would go on to be the mother of my daughter Siân. She was the friend of Gary's girlfriend and we all went to Plymouth for the weekend and after that we started going out. I was relieved to have a girlfriend because I felt like a freak to have reached the age of 20 without going out with a girl. After a while, we decided I would move out of my Army accommodation in camp and live at my girlfriend's mum's house with her and her daughter, who was about five years old at the time and was a lovely little girl. I can remember being a little shocked and impressed at how independent she was, as she would get herself up and fix her own breakfast in the mornings. Not long after I moved in, her father started proceedings to get custody as he deemed that she would be better off with him and his wife. I know now that her father really resented me then because I helped my girlfriend's case, in that I am quite well-spoken and I had a respectable job in the Army, which helped her present a better home environment for the social workers who were writing their recommendations to the court. Ultimately, they did win custody and she went to live with them.

Our relationship continued but serious arguments were common, which caused me to move back into barracks a couple of times (or 'the block' as it's known by the lads). She soon moved out of her mother's and into a shared house with another woman who had a daughter in the nearby town. I think the writing was on the wall in that it was obvious that we were unlikely to remain as a couple for too much longer and I was very close to ending our relationship for good. It was at this time that she broke the news to me that she was pregnant. It was a difficult decision but with a baby coming I decided to stay with her and see how things turned out, as I didn't really know what else to do for the best.

Demonstrating Leadership

At 22, I was a father and life was definitely becoming more complicated. I was in a difficult relationship, I was a landlord, and I was trying to progress in the Army at the same time. I attended a Detachment Commanders' course which qualifies you to be in charge of an Artillery Gun and its detachment of men which would typically be about six guys. Although I attended the course as a Lance Bombardier (LBdr) (1 stripe), you would only be able to command a gun yourself as a full Bombardier (2 Stripes) or a Sergeant (3 Stripes). I came joint top on this course and not long afterwards the Commanding Officer of the Regiment granted me special powers to be able to command a gun and its detachment, firing live ammunition whilst I was still only a LBdr. This bodes very well for a soldier if he is asked and trusted to do the job of someone one to two ranks higher.

The next career course for me to attend was a Bombardier Leadership Course which would qualify me for that promotion. Gary wasn't on it with me as he would attend this course later. This was another big test for me because just like in basic training and on my LBdr Leadership course, I would be spending the whole time with the other guys on the course (about 30) and be in direct competition with them.

To do well on a course like this you have to be amongst the fittest guys and display very good military skills, but also show that you are a leader. As I had previously shown in basic training and on my LBdr Leadership course, it was being a leader that I struggled with because I felt a lot safer not sticking my head above the parapet, where I would feel exposed and vulnerable. I still felt the shame of not earning any rank in training and also not doing well on my previous leadership course. I didn't want this to happen again, so I knew if I was to do well this time, I would have to overcome my demons. The person who comes top of their Leadership Course is nearly always promoted on the last day of it after the passing off parade. This is huge because it can accelerate you to your next rank a lot quicker than you might ordinarily do, which ultimately means more pay.

The course lasts for four weeks and there is a set syllabus for the instructors to work through and test you on. This includes things like: map reading; firing small arms such as rifles, pistols and machine guns; Nuclear Biological and Chemical (NBC) warfare drills (which is essentially drills wearing a gas mask and an NBC suit and operating as a soldier wearing that equipment); infantry soldier skills; foot drill and lots of PT. I am pleased to say that in every area we were tested, I did very well. I was by this time in my life extremely fit, so all of the physical aspects of the course allowed me to shine. I was intelligent enough to also do well at the non-physical tests, but was I displaying enough leadership skills for the instructors liking? I could sense I had the respect of the other students, but could I dare to push myself forwards more when I knew the instructors wanted people to naturally take charge? Of course, the group has to allow that person to take charge, and that's what I was most afraid of – the possibility of rejection, being shunned by everyone and being firmly put back in my place was a constant fear. One situation occurred however that got me noticed by the course officer Captain White, who had served in 7 Para RHA, which meant he had Parachute

Wings on his arm. This gained him extra respect from the men because anyone who has served in a Commando or a Parachute Regiment is clearly a driven and fit individual. We were on our final exercise in Scotland and were navigating as a course over some arduous terrain in cold, wet and windy weather. Captain White used this situation to test our mettle. He said that because of the bad weather, he would allow anyone who did not want to continue on foot to our final objective to get on to the transport; those who felt up to it could carry on with him on foot. I could tell that most of the course wanted to get on the transport but that they were afraid of being harshly judged for doing so. There was no way I was getting on that transport unless I was ordered to, so I immediately announced that I wanted to carry on and stepped to one side to allow anyone else who wanted to carry on to join me. About a third of the course came over to where I was standing, and the others stayed put. Captain White then said, "Ok you lot, get on the transport and we will see you at the final checkpoint. LBdr Poneskis you will navigate us there and let's go as I'm getting bloody cold standing around." That was my moment and I knew it. Thankfully, even though the weather was so poor, I successfully navigated us to the pick-up point where the others were waiting in the vehicles. I felt very good, because a situation had presented itself where I didn't have to say something like "Right you lot, follow me," and then hope that they did. I just had to act and think quickly which caused others to follow.

Towards the end of these leadership courses there is usually an infantry exercise, and those students who are in the running for top student are given leadership roles to perform. An infantry platoon of about 30 men will have a Platoon Commander (Plt Cdr) in charge, a Platoon Sergeant, three Corporals and six Lance Corporals. Throughout the five-day exercise, the Plt Cdr role would be given to those students who were clearly in the frame for top student, to see how they performed under pressure as the main person in charge. The last serial of the final exercise was always the final attack and whoever was given the Plt Cdr role for this was, more often than not, going to get top student on the course. As the exercise progressed, different guys who I knew were in the running were being given Plt Cdr, which caused me mixed feelings. Was I in the running at all? Time was running out and there were still several guys I considered to be 'up there' who he still hadn't given the Plt Cdr role to.

The penultimate day of exercise arrived – at which time there was only time for one more Plt Cdr, as he would have to plan the final attack. Capt White visited our Harbour Position. This is a triangular formation that an infantry platoon would adopt, typically in a wooded area, to operate out of tactically for days or even weeks. We all waited with trepidation to hear who was going to get Plt Cdr and probably come top of the course and be immediately promoted. He teased it out for what seemed like an eternity and then said, "The student who will be Plt Cdr for the final attack is LBdr Poneskis."

I was elated but I had to keep it hidden because I still had to perform well as the Plt Cdr, otherwise it meant nothing. Capt White put all of the other front runners in the other leadership roles in the Platoon (Sergeant down to LCpl). I was a little bit concerned about this because I knew that at least one of these guys resented me being in pole position, as he definitely felt that he should come top of the course. If he was also in a position of authority during this final phase, then he could potentially scupper things or even attempt to upstage me whilst I was doing my best to be in charge as the leader.

We were given the location of the enemy who were using some abandoned buildings that we had to attack at dawn the following morning,, so I went about planning the final attack meticulously. I took the Section Commanders with me to do a recce on the enemy position in order to decide how best we should attack it the next day. We spent many hours on our belt buckles, getting as close as we dared to the enemy in order to pinpoint exactly where everyone should be and how best to attack them in the morning and when exactly. This is known in the military as the H hour (the hour a combat attack is to be initiated). We also rehearsed over and over the route from the Harbour position to each section's final attack position. I wanted this to be second nature for the section commanders because when they did it again for real, it would be night time and I didn't want anyone to get lost, which would ruin the attack. I also didn't want any excuse for anyone to use a torch to lead the way or for map reading. Additionally, I didn't want anyone using their radios or even to speak to each other during our approach – all of which could give away our position and alert the enemy.

For my final rehearsal, the section commanders had to show me that at each point where their section needed to head off in a different direction to get to their attack position, they would do so without any communication necessary from me. We repeated this over and over until I was confident that even in the dark and when tired, they would still be able to do it. We then returned to the Harbour position and I had to give my orders to the platoon. The orders process is where you explain in minute detail everyone's role in the attack and there are many 'actions on' to cover. These actions on are instructions to follow if certain things happen, so that everyone knows what to do if things don't go exactly to plan. If a leader has a comprehensive list of actions on, it shows he is thinking clearly and understands the types of things that might go wrong and what to do in each instance to keep on top of the situation. Captain White made sure that he was present for my orders, as it was a difficult thing for someone to do under pressure and a good test of an individual. My fear of someone trying to upstage me in front of Captain White was justified because that's exactly what happened during my Orders. I think I only made one mistake whilst giving them, which was not repeating a 'grid location' I gave twice (which you should always do). This was a map coordinate that I had given to one of the Section Commanders to be at for the final attack. One of the other Section Commanders interrupted me and pointed out that I hadn't repeated the grid location. I hesitated for a second, as I knew he was right, but I also knew what he was up to. I decided to put him back in his place and told him that I was confident that he had got the correct grid, so I didn't need to repeat it. Of course, the other section commander knew where his attack location was; we had been there 10 times that day and I knew he also had it written down. I probably should have just repeated the grid again, but I made a snap decision not to let this guy act as though he was really in charge and more capable than me. Captain White didn't say anything, but simply observed and nodded.

After orders it was up to the section commanders to rehearse close to the Harbour position, as much as possible, on exactly what they would be doing for the final attack – what formation to travel in; who would be where and next to who; who carried what, etc. All of this was again necessary so there was no need for talking when it was done for real. After the rehearsals were complete and I was happy that everyone knew exactly what to do in the morning, we went into 'Harbour Routine' and whilst people rotated on sentry, the others ate and slept and prepared their equipment and weapons for the attack.

After what seemed like no time at all in my sleeping bag, I was woken by an off-coming sentry at reveille which was about 0400 hrs, two hours before H Hour : 0600 hrs. I knew the guys were tired at the end of a long exercise without much sleep, but I was happy that everyone seemed focussed on the task in hand. We all got packed away and into formation without any fuss, which was a relief as so far it was going to plan. Captain White turned up before we set off without telling us he would, so that he could gauge our performance. (After all, he knew exactly what time we would be leaving as he had been at my orders.)

I couldn't have been happier with how the next phase went, because the guys did in fact branch off at exactly the right place to go off in their own directions to their attack locations without any talking whatsoever. I learnt later that this caught out Captain White because he had intended to stay with me for the final attack. But without realising that we had split, he carried on walking with one of the sections before realising – at which time, it was too late for him to try to catch me up again. Each section commander knew exactly where to go, and there was no noise or torches either, which I was very happy with. Everyone was in position before H hour and we hadn't been detected by the enemy. So far so good! My signal to initiate the attack was to fire a flare over the enemy position at H hour. Apart from H hour being a little before dawn, which was a slight error on my part, everyone played their part and the attack went well and to plan. Captain White gave us all a debrief and he said he was very impressed with how it went, especially how silently we approached, which had caught him out. I felt immense relief at this point. Surely, I had done it now and surely, I would come top of the course and be the one presented with the top student award and get promoted in front of my family. I wanted it so much.

We travelled as a course back from Scotland to Larkhill to complete the final few days of the course. All that was left to do in the final few days was a Basic Fitness Test or BFT, (which is a 1.5 mile run as a squad followed by a mile and a half against the clock) and also learn and practise all of the Drill required for the Pass Off Parade in front of the families. We had already done a BFT earlier on in the course and I came first on that by some margin, so I was feeling pretty confident of my chances of staying on top.

The Fly in the Ointment

An unusual thing was about to happen though, for a course like this. One of the course Instructors had messed up and there wasn't any accommodation booked for the course to remain together during the last few days. We would still do all of the normal course program during the day, but at night each man would have to go back to his room in the block or to his Army quarter if he was married. I hadn't been to see Siân for about 10 days as we had been up in Scotland, so I went round see her. Her mum was very tired looking after Siân on her own and I offered to stay over and help, although I was very tired myself as I hadn't had much sleep for a while either. The BFT was on first thing in the morning, followed by parade rehearsal. Siân was waking up during the night as babies do, and we were both getting up to see to her. Somehow my alarm clock got knocked and switched off during the night and I overslept! When I woke, I had that instant panic feeling that you get when you are late for something very important. I leapt out of bed and looked at my watch which told me I had missed the BFT! I drove back to camp with a knot in my stomach and a feeling of dread. I got changed and into my uniform and went to meet up with the rest of the course and the instructors on the parade square where drill rehearsal was about to commence. All the other guys were wide-eyed watching me approach with faces that said, 'What have you done?'

The most likely thing that was about to happen to me was I would be thrown off the course and sent back to my sub-unit in disgrace. This would mean I would either have to wait another year to do the next 14 Regiment course or be put on a course with another regiment. Both scenarios meant I would have to go through the whole thing again and suffer a long delay in getting promoted. I just hoped that the course instructors, but more importantly Capt. White, would give me some leniency because of the cock-up with the accommodation. If there had been accommodation this would not have happened as I would have had a normal night's sleep and I would have woken with all of the other lads in the same barrack room as would usually happen on a course like this. But would this be taken into account? I know that at least one of the sergeants argued that I should be kicked off the course, but Capt. White decided to let me stay on. He gave me the news that he had intended to give me Top Student, but now he couldn't. I felt relieved and grateful at being allowed to complete the course but also completely gutted. The last couple of days mainly consisted of the rehearsals for the final parade. My mum and her husband (who himself had been a late entry captain in the Marines) were coming to see me pass off the square but they would not see me be awarded top student. After the parade, all of the students and their families assembled in the Sergeant's mess for a curry lunch to see the award of best student and most improved student (which I was happy not to receive) given by the commanding officer. The best student went up and collected his award and was also promoted. I just stayed at the back of the room with my mum feeling dejected. It was at this point a couple of people turned around and looked directly at me because someone at the front had called out my name. I made my way quizzically towards the front of the room where the CO stood with Captain

White; they had decided that although they could not give me top student, because of the mitigating circumstances they were still happy to promote me to Bombardier! I felt so happy and a huge sense of relief washed over me once again as I was handed my Bombardier rank. I still really regret not actually coming top of that course because it would have helped me exorcise the feelings of insecurity and inferiority that stayed with me for many years to come, but at least I had succeeded in getting promoted to Bombardier at the age of 22, which was younger than most guys would be at that rank.

A Dad Out of his Depth

I decided to keep a room for myself in the block which allowed me somewhere to go and stay on the occasions that Siân's mum and I fell out, which seemed to be happening more and more often. I eventually decided to end the relationship for good, but this was a very difficult time in my life because I was worried about Siân. For her sake, my mother and I decided to apply for custody. I won't go into detail, but it was one of the most traumatic things I have ever had to deal with, even taking my military service into account. On the day of the custody hearing, the judge granted full residency of Siân to us, which was another huge relief for me, because I knew in my heart that Siân would be better off living with my family.

As Siân was growing up, I struggled over how to do the best for her. Should I leave the Army, and maybe get a part-time job, that would allow me to be her main carer? My ambition was to climb the ranks and become an Army Commando and maybe even join the SAS, but if I left the Army to takeover full time from my mother, none of that could happen.

An early photo of me with Siân

Mum and Terry both reassured me that they were happy with the arrangement we had, so we continued with them having her full time, with me supporting her financially and being there as much as I could. And so, they both went on to lead the lives of parents with a young child again, many years after their own kids had flown the nest. I will always be grateful to Mum and Terry for the sacrifice they made for Siân and me at this time in our lives. I do feel guilt over Siân's upbringing in that I was in the Army throughout but I did the best I could for her, apart from actually leaving the Army. I draw comfort from the fact that Siân is now a well-rounded adult with a very good job as a Modern Languages teacher after leaving University with a degree. She is fluent in French, German and Spanish. Siân achieved this through sheer determination and hard work and she deserves enormous credit for achieving this whilst having an unconventional and often difficult upbringing.

The Next Step

At this point in my career, I reckoned if I worked hard, I could be promoted to Sergeant at about 25 years old and then apply for 29 Cdo, based in Plymouth. My mum was also planning a permanent move back to Plymouth with Siân, which would mean the two-plus hour journey to see her would be dramatically reduced. Fate was about to play its part however, because my Regiment was scheduled to be altered completely. In 1995, everyone was given a posting order telling them what Regiment they would be going to by 1996 and, coincidentally, Gary and I were both told we would be going to Regiments locally in Tidworth, Wiltshire. I was to go to 1 RHA and Gary to 19 Regt RA. Although I felt I was close to becoming a sergeant, this meant that I was not about to be promoted within 14 Regiment because everyone was allocated a slot in their new Regiment at their current rank. This was clearly my time to make my move for 29 Cdo because Mum was now also moving to Plymouth with Siân. So I could hopefully finally fulfil my ambition and get into 29 Cdo and be nearer to Siân at the same time, so I put my application in. I knew the Commando course was going to be physically very tough and although I was still pretty fit, I knew I needed to improve in certain areas. I worked a lot on my upper body strength and also did a lot of running in boots in order to get them properly broken in and to harden my feet up more to prevent blisters.

Becoming a Commando?

I arrived at The Royal Citadel Plymouth (29 Cdo's camp) which is located in a fantastic spot on Plymouth Hoe, in early October 1995, ready to do the three-week 'beat up' course prior to the eight-week Commando course. This was like being in basic training again because you run everywhere, and everybody is shouting at you! Most of the other guys who are there to do the course are not long out of basic training so this is quite normal for them, but for the few of us who had been in for a few years we just had to readjust. The beat up course consisted of a lot of endurance and cardio-vascular training, upper body strengthening and lots of climbing ropes with and without weigh/equipment. There was also fieldcraft and tactical training conducted on Dartmoor which involved staying out for several days and nights to get used to living out of a Bergan (soldier's large backpack) and operating in a cold and wet environment whilst being tested and trained as an infantry soldier. An awful lot of physical training is squeezed into these three weeks and although I was pretty fit to start with, I did find it hard at times. It does have to be hard though because the instructors need to know that each man is ready to go on to the full All Arms Commando course. So, as with any selection-type course, it has to weed out those who are not physically or mentally up to the challenge. About half of the guys who started the beat up either RTU'd (Return to Unit), themselves or had to withdraw with injury, or were not deemed ready for the

All Arms course by the instructors. About 20 of us passed that phase on the Friday and we were told to report to the Royal Marines Training Centre at Lympstone near Exmouth on Sunday. Now, we were in the hands of the Royal Marines for the next eight weeks. The Royal Marines run two main courses at Lympstone which, if you pass, will allow you to wear the coveted 'Green Beret'. The two courses are the 'Royal Marines Commando course' for Royal Marines only, and the 'All Arms Commando course' for the Army and Navy (and, on very rare occasions, the RAF), although the vast majority on the All Arms course are from the Army. If successful on their respective course, The Royal Marines, Navy Commandos and Army Commandos will then serve together in 3 Commando Brigade, performing their respective roles. The Royal Marines wear a green beret with a RM cap badge, the Navy wear a green beret with the Navy cap badge and the Army wear a green beret with the cap badge of their own Army Unit, which in my case was the Artillery. If I was successful on my AACC, I would go back to and serve in 29 Commando Regiment Royal Artillery and wear a green beret, but if unsuccessful I would go to 1 RHA in Tidworth and continue to wear a blue beret. This was not something I was prepared to contemplate as I badly wanted to become a Commando, and I also didn't want to be a 2.5-hour drive away from Siân again!

On the All Arms Cdo course, the days start very early and finish very late. There is a lot of arduous physical training, and physical tests to pass each week in order to remain on the course. One of the unofficial tests is the 'Yomp' on to the exercise area carrying all your equipment at a forced pace, and whilst on exercise if anyone on the course does anything wrong you are all subjected to punishment PT, commonly known as a 'beasting'! By all accounts, our course seemed to be getting a lot of beastings due to people breaking rules or doing something wrong, so it was a hard course to be on. There were no officer-ranked personnel (students trying to earn their green beret) on the course which was unusual; sometimes quite senior officers would attend the All Arms Course, and I am sure that the fact that we had none caused the instructors to get a little carried away at times. The most senior guys we had on the course were two staff sergeants. As well as the beastings, another requirement for a commando is the ability to do wet and dry drills. This means that you only ever wear dry clothes in your sleeping bag; you have to wear clothes even if it's warm weather in case you are 'bugged out' which means you have to get up and go very quickly (due to an enemy attack, for instance). At the same time, all of your wet clothes have to be packed away in waterproof bags (to stop the rest of your kit getting wet) in your Bergan. This may sound obvious and quite easy to do, but in cold weather on a tactical infantry exercise it isn't. It was now late November during a particularly cold spell on Dartmoor. In the evening, and prior to going into 'Harbour Routine', we were marched through a river and made to completely submerge. Once back in the Harbour, guys went on sentry for an hour at a time in each corner of the triangular position and the remainder carried out personal admin which mainly involved weapon cleaning and cooking and eating a hot meal. Being on sentry and lying still wearing soaking wet clothes in freezing temperatures was not much fun, but it was a necessary evil. This is because you have to keep your dry clothes for getting into your sleeping bag. Getting into the sleeping bag in wet clothes would mean that your clothes and bag would lose their insulating properties and you would most likely become a cold weather casualty and be a liability to yourself and others. When you come off sentry and have done your personal admin you can get out of your wet clothes and into dry ones. What comes next is the hardest because, before you know it, someone is waking you up for your turn to go on sentry and you have to get back into your wet clothes in the middle of the night on Dartmoor in freezing temperatures to do it. I can remember that my wet clothes had frozen like stiff cardboard and I had to bend them backwards and forwards to be able to open them up in order to put them on. After a very cold stint on sentry, you go through the same reverse process before getting back into your bag. In the morning, as is the case most mornings, you have a full kit inspection with everything you have laid out in a set order for the instructors to inspect for cleanliness and serviceability. If anything was found not to be in order (like a dirty mess tin or dirt or rust on your weapon), then you were told to report to the 'flank'. Once the inspection was complete and all offenders there, you were given another beasting which was usually a pretty severe one to act as a deterrent against not having good admin and ending up on the flank. It was normally the same old faces who appeared on the flank and if someone was there too often, they would be RTU'd for poor admin in the field. Most guys would feel extremely ashamed about going back to their unit with that label. Thankfully, I was rarely on the flank. After a long and cold night, it was actually a relief to get out of the Harbour position and to carry on with the programme of activity that the instructors had planned for you. I can remember that it was quite nice weather and throughout the day you could see the steam rising off the back of the man ahead as our clothes were drying out. I was really pleased about this because I knew that the night routine would be so much easier not having to change in and out of wet clothes. But this was not to be. I can't remember who did what, but someone did something wrong, and at nightfall we were punished. So, as a course we were made to totally submerge in the river again before returning back to the harbour. Punishing everyone is a much-used method in the military because it causes everyone to get on the regular offender's back, and as an individual you certainly don't want the wrath of all of your course mates on you, as well as the instructors! It's very effective at encouraging individuals to not fuck up and to try harder. As you can imagine, morale was low at this point and I am pretty sure that if there had been more senior officers on the course, we would not have been getting such harsh treatment considering the weather conditions.

The instructors seemed to have a bit of a downer on us throughout, and it genuinely seemed that they thought we were a bad lot and were not just posturing. They invited the senior instructor – who was a Major and who wouldn't normally have interacted with us at all – to address us as a course and to threaten us all with being RTU'd unless we improved our game. From what I could see, everyone seemed to be doing their best, so I couldn't understand why all the instructors were giving us such a hard time, which caused a lot of bickering and in-fighting among us, which made it a lot harder than it should have been.

A couple of significant events were going to happen to me on week five of the eight. The first serial of the week was a 12-mile load carry, which was a course 'pass or fail' test and was mainly uphill. It was quite straightforward for me – apart from the last few miles when I developed a severe pain in my left foot and I started to drop back a bit as I was finding it very difficult to maintain the fast pace whilst limping. If you drop back too much, you are placed in the 'Jack Wagon' which is the safety vehicle that picks up anyone who falls behind. This meant failing the course and there was no way I was going in the Jack Wagon so I dug really deep to stay with the squad until the end, which thankfully I did. What followed on immediately after a cup of tea in a field was a survival exercise where we had to get by with only the kit we were wearing (no bergens, warm kit or food) and a survival tin which contains a fire lighting kit, a fishing kit and snares for catching things to eat. We were split into small groups and told to go and make our survival shelters to live in, which would be our homes for the week. We were allowed to use the exercise area to forage for anything that might help in a survival scenario such as plastic sheeting to help to waterproof yourself and your shelter. Unless it was an emergency, we were not allowed to cross the road which surrounded the area which was our outer perimeter. This was to ensure that guys didn't go and bother any people living nearby looking for food or materials. To discourage any one from doing this, we were warned that if anyone was caught going out of the area, we would all be beasted together as a course. I was hoping that I had only strained my foot and it would get better but, unfortunately, I was starting to limp on it more and more. Apart from the pain in my foot and feeling a little cold and hungry, I quite enjoyed this exercise as we were taught and had to put in to practice, certain survival skills, as well as day and night navigation techniques without the use of a map and compass. In the shelter at night, you forget about your usual inhibitions and you cuddle together in the spoon position to keep warm, hoping that the guy behind you isn't enjoying the experience a little too much.

One evening, a safety flare went off in the middle of the exercise area which meant that everyone had to go to the centre to meet up with the instructors. Upon arrival, I could see that the DS were not in a good mood at all and this caused my heart to sink, because whatever had happened, I really didn't want to get a beasting with such a sore foot. We were told that a local farmer had reported to the instructors that two guys had knocked on his door asking for food.

This clearly meant that these two guys had crossed the road and left the exercise area, even though it had been forbidden and the consequences explained. I was a little confused, but relieved however because we were told that if the two guys in question owned up, that only those two would be punished and not everyone else. Everyone looked around to see who would come forward, but no one did. The DS said that if no one came forward that we would all get beasted until whoever it was owned up, but still no one did. A lot of bickering and shouting started among the course and the DS. Most of us turned towards the Staff Sergeants, who were the senior among us, to show some leadership and to convince the culprits to come forward. One of the SSgts seemed to take the lead in demanding that whoever it was came forward. It was now raining quite heavily and we were all getting wet, which was going to make for a very cold night indeed unless we could get back to our shelters very soon. Despite his demands that someone should own up, no one came forward and after a lot of threatening, the DS said, 'Right, that's enough: everyone get fell in over there for a beasting.' I was gutted as I limped over for this, and I couldn't believe whoever was responsible could allow all of their course mates to get this beasting because of what they had done, especially as we were cold, wet and hungry and some of us were clearly carrying injuries. At last, two guys came forward and said, "Staff it was us." But strangely, the DS said, "Bullshit, no it wasn't, fall back in." Now I was really confused: what on earth was going on? The DS said, "Right, if whoever did it won't own up, then, by the front, double march!" At this point a young Gunner put his hand up and said it was him. Everyone stood silent and stared at him, and at the DS who seemed to accept that it might be him. What happened next shocked me completely, because the person who then also came forward and said, "it was me" was the SSgt who moments earlier had been shouting at all of us, "Whoever has done it come forward now!" I was in utter disbelief and at this point the DS said, 'Yes we know it was you." Two lads who were actually innocent had put their hands up, prepared to take the beasting for the sake of the rest of us. What made the DS sure of their identities, was the description from the farmer and the fact that the SSgt was so very distinctive that there was no one else who could match the description. Unbelievably, it took the very young Gunner to come forward first before the SSgt did. He must have been bewildered trying to decide what to do in the minutes before he owned up and must have been looking towards the SSgt to take the lead; after all, it would have been him that made the decision to go to the farm in the first place as he was extremely senior compared to the Gunner.

All the DS knew from the outset was that it was the SSgt and most likely one other from his small shelter group. The DS decided that the behaviour that the SSgt displayed warranted more than a beasting and decided to RTU him from the course. I completely agree that this was an appropriate punishment because he displayed an extreme lack of integrity throughout this episode; he was inviting others to take the rap for him and was prepared to allow people who were injured to get a beasting until someone else owned up. Unfortunately, they also RTU'd the Gunner which I thought was very unfair, because he would not have dared to argue against the SSgt when he undoubtedly suggested going to the farm, and any other young Gunner would have done the same. The fact that he was the first out of the two to own up, in a highly stressful and confusing situation for him, showed guts and integrity. As far as I am concerned, he should have remained on the course.

As we returned to our shelters, we were only sad under the circumstances that he had gone and we remained gobsmacked that the SSgt had behaved so poorly. It was generally known that if you were RTU'd from the course due to a lack of integrity, then you would not be allowed to return on a future course. We were sure that this would apply to the SSgt but what of the Gunner? Surely, he would be allowed back on due to mitigating circumstances? As we settled down for the night in our shelters, we knew we would just have to wait and see.

The rest of the survival exercise went without too much incident, but my foot did not get any better. I was sure I had just pulled a muscle or strained something, and I just hoped that it would improve before the next physical event or beasting occurred.

After the survival phase, the next serial on the course was a trip to Poole in Dorset to receive some training on using Rigid Raiders, which are military speed boats operated primarily by Royal Marines, and the two types of amphibious landing craft used within the Commando Brigade. Although it wasn't a physically demanding day, we did have to jump from boat to boat whilst moving at a speed which was very painful on my bad foot.

The other painful part of the day was practising a drill which involved dragging a rigid raider (which weighs about a tonne) across deep and soft mud to get it back into the water after it had been intentionally 'beached' by the coxswain.

We finished our day at Poole and made our way back to Lympstone. I decided to visit the sick bay on camp, which is a military version of a GP's surgery, to see if they could give me some anti-inflammatory medicine or maybe the medics could strap my foot up to ease the pain. I was told that my metatarsal bone in my foot was broken, and it was too severe to allow me to remain on the course. I was gutted by this news; I tried to argue against their decision but the doctor, although sympathetic, would not relent. She explained that if it had only been a hairline, they would have considered it but not a complete fracture. The sick bay informed the training team that they must RTU me immediately. This was very hard for me to take. I had to pack up all my stuff and say goodbye to my friends. Most of them would go on to pass the course in a couple of weeks before Christmas leave and return to 29 Cdo with their green berets. I went back on crutches, knowing that it would be many months before my foot would be healed enough for me to start another beat up and to go back to Lympstone for another attempt at passing.

Crap Hat

The months that followed were not nice at all. There is a big divide in a commando regiment between Cdo-trained guys who wear the commando dagger badge and a green beret; at the time Cdo-trained guys even wore a different uniform to non-commando trained lads. The non-commando trained guys (or 'NCT's) would be nicknamed 'Crap Hats', which would often simply be shortened to 'Hat'. This was a reference to the fact that the blue, general-issue beret was considered to be crap in comparison to a green commando one. The commando-trained lads would often simply refer to you as 'Hat' or 'Harry' (which is short for 'Harry the Hat'). Some guys, not all, would actually display a level of animosity towards 'hats' that could be a little too intense at times, and it created an environment where someone like me felt completely alienated. Most guys in the regiment wouldn't take this name-calling and ribbing too far, but simply use it as a tool to motivate NCTs to push themselves harder to get their green beret in order to gain acceptance. I think this mentality does have its merits if it is used for a short time, like the time you are on your 'beat up' course at the Citadel prior to going to Lympstone.

However, if you are forced to live with this regime for months on end, it starts to really get to you. Unfortunately, as is human nature, some people use this extra power as a bullying tool. The thing that made this situation more complex for me was that I was a Bombardier with two stripes on my arm, so rank-wise I was senior or equal in rank to about two-thirds of the regiment. Under normal circumstances, a Bombardier in a Regiment would have a certain level of respect and authority over Gunners and Lance Bombardiers. The fact that I was a crap hat though made for blurred lines as far as who was senior to who, and as I mentioned earlier, some of the guys exploited this opportunity to challenge me and even deliberately attempt to humiliate me in order to satisfy their own ends.

I was feeling the same way I did when I was isolated at boarding school again and I felt really uncomfortable on a daily basis. It was a very unhappy time for me, and my self-confidence and self-esteem dropped to rock bottom. I just wanted to fast forward to when I could get back to Lympstone and get my beret, so that I wouldn't have to feel like such an outcast any more. I applied for permission to live out of camp in my own flat which would enable me to see much more of Siân, and thankfully I was granted permission, which was a blessed relief for me. Gradually, my foot got better and I was able to get back into proper training again. Things were about to become complicated however, because a new Sergeant took over the Cdo training at the Citadel. He was old school and I know that he strongly disagreed that someone like me could arrive at the Regiment and keep his rank. He definitely did not want me in the regiment and he did everything in his power to make life as hard for me as he could.

On one occasion he conducted an accommodation inspection at 0800 hours. I attended it as the most senior NCT, with a notebook and pencil, in order to follow him around and take notes on any issues he picked up on, so that I could brief all of the other NCTs living in the block, which was normal. When he arrived for the inspection, he spoke to me with his usual venomous tone as he asked, "Do you live in this fucking accommodation?" I replied, "No Sergeant." He told me to, "Fuck off out then, because you've got no fucking right to be here." I duly did as I was told and waited outside for the inspection to finish, which lasted about half an hour.

The following week, as published on *Daily Orders,* there was to be another block inspection at 0800 followed by parade at 0830. I didn't make the same mistake of attending the block inspection and decided to wait outside, out of his way. The block inspection started on time at 0800, so I chatted outside with a couple of other NCTs that also had permission to live out. We didn't really need to be there at 0800 as the block inspection wasn't for us, but we decided to be 'around' just in case. At about 0810 I decided to go and get my notebook which I had left in my car. When I came back at about 0815, the block inspection had finished early and everyone was on parade in three ranks being addressed by the Sgt. As soon as I walked over, he said, "You're late for parade, warned for office" – which meant I would be charged and face disciplinary action. I wanted to say that I had been there earlier and just went to get my notebook and that on orders it actually stated that parade time was 0830. But he cut me off immediately saying, "Shut the fuck up: no buts, this is a one-way conversation. You are warned for office, now get fucking fell in!" which meant join the others in the ranks. I did what I was told hoping that when he thought it through, he would realise that he was not being fair. But I was wrong. He pursued the charge thoroughly and I had to go on Battery Orders for being late for parade. The only thing I could be charged with was being late for the

08:30 parade because the previously published orders clearly stated that only those living in the NCT accommodation should be on parade for 08:00. I could have proved without a shadow of doubt that I was not late for the 08:30 parade but my dilemma was that I didn't dare contest the charge. I already felt he had it in for me and if I discredited him, it could have got a lot worse. At the time, I didn't know if I would be allowed to go back to Lympstone to complete the Cdo course, and he could do a lot to make that not happen, so I decided to simply take it on the chin.

When the Battery Commander who was a Major asked if I was guilty of missing the 08:30 parade, I pleaded guilty. His punishment, which I felt was extremely harsh, was to fine me £900 to be taken in one hit from my wages, which was nearly all of my monthly wage! I can remember feeling stunned at his 'award' and a little bit sick. I had a mortgage and bills to pay and a daughter to support. This was so very wrong. I don't want to alarm people into thinking that this type of injustice is commonplace in the armed forces, because I know for a fact that it isn't. I just happened to be caught up in a very unusual situation that allowed someone to get away with an abuse of power and I chose not to challenge it for my own reasons.

The Entrepreneur is Born

I now had to think of a way that I could make some money – and fast! My brother was working for a company that sold really expensive vacuum cleaners that retailed at around £1000. I am not going to mention the name and I don't know what they are like now, but certainly at the time they were 'all singing all dancing' ones that had awesome suction power. These machines could also shampoo your carpet and sofas and had a compressor so you could use the spray-gun for different purposes or even use it to inflate paddling pools. These machines were not sold in the shops but on referrals from people who had either bought a machine or had a demonstration and provided names and numbers of their friends and family who might be interested. With these referrals the tele-sales staff would call and book appointments for a sales rep to go around and clean the carpet, demonstrating what the machine could do and try to convince the householder to buy one. Whether the machine was bought or not, the rep would ask for referrals and on it would go. At my brother's firm the sales reps worked on a commission-only basis, so they had to sell to earn money. I asked my brother Johnny if he could teach me how to do the demos to see if I could earn myself some money. Johnny sent me out to shadow some of the other reps outside of my normal working hours. Unfortunately, none of the demos I watched, which seemed to go really well, resulted in a sale and so it was hard to see how this was going to work for me. After watching only a few demos, my brother asked if I wanted to go on a few appointments myself. I was shocked at how soon he wanted to put me out there on my own, and I didn't feel at all ready, but I needed to try to make some money as soon as possible so I nervously agreed. I was given my own machine for demos and a brand new one (in case I sold), and off I went to my first appointment after I finished work at camp. I was really nervous because I didn't really have a good working knowledge of the machine or the demonstration. I can remember stumbling through the demo somehow and unsurprisingly didn't sell it. I felt really drained afterwards due to all the nervous energy I used up and I called my brother to tell him it was over. In a matter-of-fact way he said, "Ok, fine" and proceeded to give me the name and address of the next appointment. It was now 8pm and I tried to argue that I was knackered and needed to get home to rest and prepare for work in camp the next day, but he was having none of it. So, I went to the next appointment which was a nice house with nice cars outside. The owner, who had his own car sales company, was very self-assured and he made it very clear that he was in charge and I would do as I was told in his house. He already knew how the process worked and that I would try and sell him the machine but he said he would not be buying it full stop and he just wanted his rug cleaned as promised over the phone. He had a big dog which slept on its own rug which is what they wanted to be cleaned. The rug stank of wet dog and was covered in hair but I did a pretty good job of cleaning it up. After I had done this, the man was pleased but as it was late, he wanted me to go and not bother doing the demonstration because there was no point as he wouldn't be buying. It was very tempting to just agree, but something in me decided to push on and ask him if I could please go ahead and do it, as it would help me learn and it was my job, etc, and so he agreed. I spent another 30 minutes on the demo and made a few less mistakes that time although it was still a bit of a car crash. Something weird happened though: the home owner seemed genuinely interested in buying the machine. He asked me if there was a payment plan and what the interest rate was if he took out credit to buy it. He then asked me a question which I just didn't understand at all, which was: 'Is the interest rate fixed or variable?' I said, 'I think it's fixed,' but seeing that I was unsure and because he was someone who deals with finance agreements all the time, he asked to see the credit agreement form and it clearly stated that it was variable! At this point, I decided to call my brother who would always man the phone in the office whilst his reps were doing demonstrations, as he would often need to answer questions the reps weren't sure of or speak to the clients to try to close the sale if there was one to be had. Johnny convinced the man to go ahead, decided the price that would be paid, (because this was negotiable) to have the brand-new machine that was in my boot and the man gave the phone back to me. Johnny confirmed the price I should put on the form and said, "Well done you've sold your first one already!" which made me feel thrilled and elated.

I filled out the credit agreement and set up the new machine in the house and left on cloud nine. I would earn £150 from my evening's work and for a young lad in 1996, this was a lot of money. The excitement soon waned though because the little voices in my head started and I couldn't help thinking that it was probably just a fluke and I got lucky, and most people wouldn't have the money to buy one.

Over the next month when I had some spare time in the evenings or weekends, I would call Johnny to be given any spare appointments that the full-time reps couldn't do, as they had to be given priority. Going in to people's houses like this was a real eye-opener and I couldn't believe how some people live. I completed about 12 appointments and after some cancellations and with Johnny's help, I actually sold six machines, with my total commission coming in at £1100. Johnny came to see me to give me my money whilst I was on guard duty and standing in uniform with my rifle on the main entrance to the Royal Citadel. He put the £1100 into my hand which was a huge relief because otherwise I would have defaulted on my mortgage and other bills.

I did the occasional appointment for Johnny after this and sold the odd machine but it tailed off partly because I didn't need the money as much any more and also because my training and Army activity was now intensifying and so I had less time on my hands. Looking back on this time, I know I learnt an awful lot about myself and the people whose houses I visited. A couple of these people bought a machine from me but they couldn't really afford it, and if I am to be completely honest with myself, I knew at the time that they were making a mistake financially in signing the credit agreement form and I feel guilty about it to this day.

Second Go at All Arms

Now that I had got my finances back on track, and with my foot feeling better, I could focus on getting fit so that I could get back on the All Arms Course. Earlier in the year the RTU'd SSgt and Gunner were both allowed to go back to Lympstone to complete the course. At the time of writing, the Gunner is a well-respected Warrant Officer in 29 Cdo and has had a fine and honourable career in the Regiment. I have to admit that I was not pleased to see the SSgt go back and then return wearing his Cdo beret whilst I was still injured and struggling. The SSgt had also been promoted to Warrant Officer during this time. This is because he had already been on his Gunnery Career Course prior to going to 29 Cdo – his promotion had already been scheduled by the wider Artillery and so it was not 29 Cdo's decision. This was not popular with the majority of the Regiment because he was posted in, achieved his commando status and assumed the role of a WO2 in the Regiment. I obviously have sympathy with him here because ultimately, he was only doing what people on high had deemed possible and he had not made the rule which allowed him to do it, as was the case with me.

I would not see much of him for a while as he was posted away, and in the meantime I had to get my own green beret. As soon as I was fit again, I badgered my Sgt to let me go back to Lympstone and eventually he agreed and let me go. A summer course was certainly a lot easier to a winter one that's for sure, and the general atmosphere on this course was an awful lot better also. There were several officers on the course, some of whom were quite senior, and I can only conclude that this kept things from getting out of hand. I can honestly say that compared to my first course, this was a lot easier. I enjoyed being away from the NCT regime at the Citadel because I felt accepted again and worthy.

The final commando test before being awarded the Green Beret is the 30-mile forced march across Dartmoor in less than eight hours carrying 21 lbs of kit and an SA80 rifle which weighed about 11 lbs. A safety bergen (with sleeping bag and spare clothing and medical equipment) would also be taken and guys would take turns in carrying it. On its own, this is quite a tough test but coming at the end of an arduous course conducted mostly 'in the field' (in this case, outdoors on exercise areas like Dartmoor) people can be pretty run down by this time which inevitably makes it much harder. I was feeling physically strong at this point, however, so I completed it relatively easily. I did have a bit of a scare very near the end when one of the DS pointed out that one of the guys who was taking his turn carrying the safety bergen had dropped quite far behind and he was in danger of not getting to the end in time. I made the split decision to double-back to where he was to take the bergen off him and help him get to the end in time. I can remember thinking, "Oh fuck, what have I done?" when it became obvious that we were now really up against the clock to get in on time. If we did not make it, we would not be getting our berets that day, but given the chance of doing it again the next day! It was a scary and pretty tiring ten minutes until we got to the finish line and were told we had both made it. And that was it! I had passed the Commando course at last, and in a few minutes, on that piece of moorland on Dartmoor, I would be awarded my Green Beret!

I was overwhelmed with relief more than anything. There had been plenty of hurdles (and people) to overcome along the way but it was now done at last.

We were given a few days off before reporting back to the training wing. I didn't see my Sgt, but one of the other training team NCOs told me that I was to be posted to 8 Battery which was one of the two Light Gun Batteries based at the Royal Citadel in Plymouth. I was just glad that I could go back to being a normal soldier in a Gun Battery again and not be treated like a raw recruit any more. It was nearly a year since I had arrived at the gates of 29 Cdo Regiment, and finally I could return to being a Bombardier in a Gun Detachment and be treated like an adult again!

The Journey to Depression

Unfortunately, my confidence that everything was now going to be ok was short lived. At 0800 hrs on the Monday morning, I was told to report to the 8 Battery Sergeant Major (BSM) in order to introduce myself, before being introduced to the rest of the Battery as a new member. I expected some words of wisdom from him along the lines of "work hard and keep your nose clean and you will be ok," but I actually got something completely different! His exact words, which I will never forget were, "I fought tooth and nail to stop you coming to my Battery but I was overruled." He went on to inform me that he had two Lance Bombardiers in the Battery that he wanted to promote to Bombardier and that he could only now promote one of them because I had been forced upon him and he was very angry about it. He told me I would be the number one of B Sub (this is a nickname for the Detachment Commander of detachment 2 of 6 detachments in the Battery) and told me to march out, which I did. I felt a sinking feeling and dread at the same time. This was the

Battery Sergeant Major who would have the most influence and control over my life telling me that he didn't want me and he resented my presence. I suddenly thought, "If he is this resentful about this, how must the guys in the Battery feel?" I was about to find out. The BSM shouted for a Bombardier who had been waiting in the corridor to come into the office. He told him to show me around the Battery lines and finish at B Sub's store, where the men who would be under my command in B sub would be. "Yes sir," he said, and just started walking along the corridor and down the stairs, and so I followed. He did not look at me or engage in any sort of conversation or small talk at all. He walked and I followed and whenever we walked past anything that related to 8 Bty he just pointed at it and said what it was. This went on for about 15 minutes until we arrived at the gun shed which is the hangar where the Battery's 6 Guns and their respective stores are kept and would predominantly be my place of work whilst in camp from now on. He left me at the B Sub's cage (gun store) and just walked away without saying anything else, now that he had finished his task of giving me a guided tour.

There were a couple of guys waiting there who I would soon find out were members of my gun sub or detachment which was also nicknamed a 'gun crew', but just like the Bombardier, they had no intention of being friendly and were rude. Under normal circumstances when a new Gun Number One is posted into a Battery and he would meet his gun crew for the first time, the guys would want to make a good impression, as they would be meeting their immediate boss for the first time. These guys did not care at all about creating a good first impression with me and it was humiliating. I felt so uncomfortable at this time and as I write it's giving me a knot in my stomach just thinking about it. I should have been assertive and challenged this poor and ultimately insubordinate behaviour but I didn't. I really wanted to but I just felt completely out of my depth and isolated. I could not summon any confidence and I just wanted to get out of there and be somewhere else. This was to be the start of a long road towards being accepted in 8 Battery and finding my feet.

Things were to get a lot worse for me before they got better, and I would go on to become very depressed over the coming year or so. What the BSM did at this time and in the months and years to come is something I have not managed to forgive him for yet. I know he made his contempt towards me common knowledge and as far as I am concerned, he ultimately encouraged and invited the whole Battery to shun me, and I believe he did this to satisfy the resentment he felt because I was posted in to his battery against his wishes and it interfered with his plans. I now know that he should have been much more professional than that, and that his actions were ultimately detrimental to morale and the cohesion of his Battery, which certainly damaged the operational effectiveness of the Unit. I cannot blame the BSM entirely for the reception I received in 8 Bty however. I later learned from a Gunner in the Battery called Kenny that my old Sgt, who had a lot of influence as he was quite a big personality in the Regiment, had spread the word that I was, let's say, a 'wrong un' and people should give me a wide berth.

I had met Kenny when he was going through his Commando training and he went on to pass and get his beret before me and join 8 Bty. He asked me not to tell anyone that he had told me as he didn't want to be ostracised as well. I promised not to tell anyone and I thanked him for letting me know, as this actually made me feel a lot better because as well as the BSM's actions there was another person causing me to be treated like such an outcast. Another reason I was being treated badly was due to my inability at the time to handle the situation and stand up for myself. I avoided confrontation at all costs, but it just made things worse. I would do certain jobs myself instead of delegating them to a Gunner or Lance Bombardier (which is what I should have done) because I was afraid of being ignored or worse. I am ashamed to say that on the odd occasion when I did muster the courage to ask a subordinate to do a job, I would be told, "Do it yourself you fucking hat." Even though I was now also a Commando wearing a green beret, I was still being treated and spoken to as if I was a hat because everyone was convinced that I didn't deserve to wear the beret and I had somehow faked or cheated my way to getting one; and the general consensus was that I definitely should not have kept my rank. As I have mentioned earlier, there was a common view that someone in my position should actually revert to a Gunner and at the very least revert to Lance Bombardier as had happened in the past to others.

On the occasions when I was told to "fuck off you hat" by guys junior to me, I would freeze and look to the floor and hope that no one had noticed because I didn't want others to see it and be encouraged to speak to me like it as well. I am cringing just thinking about it again because I am so embarrassed to admit that I was so feeble and weak at this time in my life. Of course, everyone nearby did notice and it just encouraged others to join in who could see my weakness, and so the situation got worse for me. Not everyone joined in with this behaviour I have to say, but they just didn't get involved and kept out of it. The Senior Non-Commissioned Officers in the Battery who might have intervened just seemed to turn a blind eye to what was going on. I know in hindsight that it was not easy for them because they also did not want to side with me or help me because that would be going against the BSM who also had a big say in their careers – so, if there was anyone who could turn this situation around it would have to be me. I wish I could say that I turned things around and proved myself quickly, but the fact is that I didn't. I fell into a depression, which I think had been lurking in the background for some time. It seems that in terms of coping, I was no longer able to keep my head above water and so I sank to a point where I became a totally dysfunctional person.

I started to drink too much, I smoked, and I could no longer think straight or organise myself at all. My flat became a mess and I would not allow anyone inside because it was so bad. My lack of self-confidence even crossed over into how I behaved around Siân, because my fear of confrontation meant that if she challenged a decision I made on what she could or couldn't do, as all two-year-olds do, I actually felt intimidated by her as well. It was lucky for me (and her) that my mother and Terry had Siân living with them as I would not have been able to cope very well with her for long periods on my own at this time.

Now that I was in an operational unit, I knew that I would soon be deploying overseas. A few months after joining the Regiment, my Battery would go on an eight-month 'seaborne' tour called Exercise Ocean Wave to the Far East and Africa. The prospect of this tour filled me with complete dread and fear because I knew that there would be no respite or escape from those who made me feel so low, as I would no longer be able to 'leave camp' to escape and hide in my flat each evening. I would be living and working in close proximity with the rest of the Battery 24/7 for the whole eight-month duration. This was going to be one of the biggest challenges of my life.

Life-Changing Tour

The tour duration was to coincide with Britain handing back Hong Kong to the Chinese in the summer of 1997. The British government decided that it would be sensible to have a seaborne military presence in the region at the time, presumably in case any sudden evacuation of people was required if things did not go according to plan! We would go with 40 Commando Royal Marines and other Commando sub units along with the Royal Navy and Royal Fleet Auxiliary. The British military decided that this would be a good opportunity to spend a considerable length of time in the region in order to conduct as much training as possible in jungle environments in the Far East. The training in Africa was to take place after the Hong Kong takeover and would last about six weeks finishing in August. We set sail from the military port of Marchwood near Southampton in early January 1997, on board the Royal Fleet Auxiliary ship *Sir Geraint*. The ship was an LSL class which is a Landing Ship Logistics vessel specifically designed to have quite a flat hull to enable it to get close to shore to facilitate amphibious landings. The ship was a military version of a roll-on roll-off ferry with both bow and stern doors to allow quick loading and unloading of vehicles and equipment.

The ship itself was nearing the end of its working life at this time and I can remember thinking that it looked like a bit of an old tub. I was shocked at how small the ship was and how cramped the living space was inside. Our accommodation was called a Mess Deck and it is where over 30 of us would be spending a lot of the next eight months together. Those of us over six feet tall had to be careful in the mess deck not to bang our heads on the ceilings, especially where the vents and sprinklers were fitted, so it felt pretty claustrophobic. Our beds were bunk beds and there were 3 beds in each one. As you can imagine, this did not give each man much bed space, considering the height of the ceiling! We had one small locker each and our remaining kit and equipment had to be kept packed away in bags for when it was required.

Living on board a ship is all about being clean, tidy, well-organised and adhering to a strict routine at all times. This is especially necessary when a lot of people are living together in such a confined space. The other issue with living with people in a confined space is that if certain people do not like you being there, it can be a very uncomfortable place to be indeed. I was really struggling and finding it hard to keep it together emotionally. One of the things that could be done was to hang a couple of towels across the space between the mattress above which would obscure you from view of anyone else in the room. This was a god send to me because everyone did it in order to catch up on sleep or just to chill. I did it to hide.

The days were filled with a combination of lectures on Jungle Warfare (the practical would come later) and general military skills, PT, servicing and maintaining our equipment, cleaning the mess deck, toilets or 'heads', showers and corridors, kitchen or galley fatigues. Essentially, this was helping the chefs before, during, and after meal times and mainly involved scrubbing pots, pans and plates in the kitchen which was uncomfortable work as the heat would get pretty unbearable in this combined space; the air con on board was definitely not up to the task, especially in the hot climate we were in. The nickname we gave to Galley fatigues was 'Viet Pan'!

We also did Watch duties which involved manning the phones in the military office and performing admin tasks, and what we called 'Dolphin Watch' which involved sitting at the back of the ship and keeping an eye on the ship's wake in case anyone fell overboard and to alert the ship's crew. When not doing these things, I would hide behind my towels as much as possible. I know now that the unfriendly treatment I was getting from a lot of the guys was not actually that bad and if the same happened to me now I would be able to put a stop to it or just brush it off as their problem not mine. As I have said previously though, I was simply vulnerable and this just encourages those people with bullying-type tendencies. I am sure that many of the guys who didn't have an issue with me just thought I was plain weird and this didn't help me make friends. Those who did have an issue with me were openly hostile and unkind, and I just felt so helpless and alone.

One of the worst incidents that happened was down to a magazine that a couple of the more senior Junior NCOs decided to produce called the *Battery Buzz*. These two guys were essentially the editors and would have the final say on what could and couldn't be written and published. When I say magazine, it was actually just a few pages of text stapled together with a bit of artwork on the front cover. It was intended to be a light-hearted publication where people could anonymously make fun of each other by writing 'piss takes' about whoever on board seemed most deserving of a good ribbing. By and large, this is exactly what it was and I found some of the pieces to be really funny, especially when it was SNCOs or Officers who were being made fun of! Unfortunately, I was to be targeted by an article and there was no intent on being funny at all. It went basically along the lines of, "This fucking Crap Hat should not be allowed to come here and steal someone else's rank. Nobody likes him or wants him around and he should just fuck off back to 'Hatland' where he belongs" It went on and on ... I was absolutely horrified reading it because I knew that every single member of the Battery from Gunner to Battery Commander would also read it. I can remember feeling really hurt that the 2 JNCOs would allow it to go to print. I am pretty sure that neither of them actually wrote it because it was not their style and they were a lot more articulate than the person who had written it. But why did they (as editors) allow something that was firstly, not funny and, secondly, so mean, unnecessary and unkind? Every other article at least intended to be funny but this was completely different: this was just nasty. Nothing was done by the hierarchy of the Battery to intervene either. This would have been the BSM's remit to clamp down on such bullying and victimisation but unsurprisingly, considering his opinion on the subject, he did nothing.

I am not saying that I didn't have good moments during this tour because I did, and there were some guys who did make more of an effort to try and get to know me. The problem was that for most of the time I simply was not acting normally and it was hard for people to get to know the real me and to see me as a friend.

This was to be a very long eight months, but I am glad to say that I learnt a lot about myself and others during this time. The trip itself was fascinating in terms of how many countries we visited and for that reason, as well as being one of the hardest times of my life, it was also the most interesting time I spent in my 24 years in the Army.

From Marchwood, we sailed through the Bay of Biscay which was a very rough crossing. Due to the fact that an LSL is so flat bottomed, it caused the ship to sway a lot from side to side under normal sailing conditions, never mind in turbulent sea conditions! As this was only day 2 of our voyage it made many of us feel extremely sea sick, but fortunately I wasn't too bad. After a while on board ship, even those people who are susceptible to sea sickness tend to get their sea legs in the end. But this early on, it was a baptism of fire!

One thing that I found to be extremely alarming was the huge impacts I could feel against the side of the ship whilst I was in my bunk. The side of the hull was thin enough to flex in and out if subjected to enough force and this is exactly what was happening. I was almost ejected out of my bed at one point which was scary at the time. What I didn't know was that a Mexeflote was attached to the side of the ship, and in the high seas it was this that was crashing against the side of the hull causing such violent bangs and impacts, and not huge waves which was what I thought at the time! A Mexeflote is essentially a floating pontoon with an engine to propel it along. When it's not possible to dock ashore, once lowered from the side, the 'mexe' can be driven to the front or back of a ship and, once secured, vehicles and men can simply pass from the ship to the mexe which can then transfer its cargo ashore or to another vessel if required. So, it was this pretty large and heavy piece of kit that was scaring me to death that second night!

After the Bay of Biscay, we passed Gibraltar and into the Mediterranean Sea. Disappointingly, we didn't get to go ashore in Gibraltar as it was too early into the voyage, but I would get to go there several times later on in my career; I even got to parachute into Gibraltar harbour which was great fun.

Our first stop in Port was the Greek island of Crete. As was the case in most of the ports we visited, we were allowed shore leave. This basically meant that we all went out 'on the town' or 'on the lash' which is another more commonly used naval slang term. This first excursion ashore was pretty eventful for a number of reasons. A huge fight occurred between my unit (8 Bty) and A (Alpha) Company (Coy) who we were sharing a ship with. On board, A company occupied the starboard side and we were on the port side. As with all military units, there is always a lot of rivalry with another unit and this was no exception. The main issue in play was that A Coy are a Royal Marine unit and 8 Bty are an Army Commando unit, so there was a definite Army vs. Royal Marine divide. This rivalry was a lot more evident in the younger guys on both sides and seemed to disappear as guys got more mature and sensible. So, once all of these young guys were allowed off the confines and strict discipline of the ship and then filled full of alcohol, it was almost inevitable that a fight or two was going to happen. Before I had any beer, I called my mum from a pay-phone to check in and to see how Siân was. I can remember that phone call very clearly because I couldn't even hold a conversation properly because my brain felt like mush. I tried to sound upbeat so that my mum wouldn't worry too much about me, but I remember not being very coherent and I actually found holding a conversation difficult. After hanging up the phone, I went into the pub and started to drink as well. A couple of the guys did speak to me that night, so I didn't feel too much like a loner. Quite early on in the night, the alcohol had quite an effect on me and I actually fell asleep. Instead of waking me up, all of the blokes left the pub and went elsewhere. This is quite a common thing for guys to do in this situation as it's a prank that is played on someone if they fall asleep drunk. Much worse fates can befall someone who falls asleep in the bar, such as losing your eyebrows or even having the front part of your hair shaved off, which is called a 'robocop' – so you shouldn't read too much into it. But imagine how I felt when I woke up on my own in that bar with all of the locals staring at me with either distain or amusement. I didn't know where all the others had gone and I was too embarrassed to go and look for them, so I simply got a cab back to the ship on my own which was pretty expensive, as it had been a coach ride from the port to the town. It was the next day that I learned of the mass brawl that had taken place later on in the town. It had all kicked off between 8 Bty and Alpha Coy and by all accounts it was like a fight in the Wild West, with people being thrown through the bar windows. Of course, bragging rights of who won this fight would not be agreed on, but one of the medics who was on duty in the sick bay on board who treated the walking wounded, said that there were an awful lot more Royal Marines being treated than our lot. So I am bound to say that my lot won! Further evidence was the fact that I didn't notice any of our guys with any visible injuries but there were plenty of shiners in evidence from the starboard side the next day! In all seriousness, I think this was a seminal moment on the tour because we did get on much better with the Royal Marines after the fight for whatever reason. I believe that, similar to the Parachute Regiment or 'Para's, Royal Marines are indoctrinated during their training to believe that they are the hardest of men and they can look down their noses at anyone from other military units. Most of the Royals who were fighting were really young guys not long out of Civvy Street, and training and their average age would have been a few years less than that of our guys. I am sure that these young Royal Marines would have fared a lot better against a normal Army unit who would probably have felt intimidated by them – but not with 8 Bty. An Army Commando is someone who strives to get into a much tougher Army unit physically, in this case 29 Cdo, and only the more determined and able will earn that right, so you end up with a pretty tough collection of men. Army Commandos do have a healthy respect for Royal Marines, but the friction occurs when this is not reciprocated. After the fight, I think most of A Coy did now respect the Bty, so thankfully, this mutual respect made for a much better co-existence on board for the remainder of the tour and there were no more mass brawls!

One funny story that I heard about that night involved a couple of our lads, Den and Bo. Obviously, I am not condoning this, but having run out of money they did a runner from their taxi in front of the Greek Navy sentry who was manning the gate into the port. The Greek soldier attempted to intercept them, but Bo sidestepped him first and with a right hook knocked him out at the same time. All hell broke loose and all of the Greek guard force, as well as the Royal Marines Police (RMP – not to be confused with Royal Military Police who are Army), were now mobilised to try and catch them. Meanwhile, they were running around in the shadows, trying to evade capture and make it back to the ship. Apparently, their cunning drunken plan was to swap jackets as this would obviously fool their pursuers! Unsurprisingly, they did not get away. The RMP were waiting for them at the top of the gangway, which is the ramp from shore to ship. A brief interrogation identified them as the guilty parties and they were told to 'Stand By' which is a naval term for: *you are in the shit and you will soon find out what's going to happen to you*! It was now that I found out that Bo was identified as being a very good soldier by the BSM and all of the hierarchy. I liked Bo a lot because he was one of the guys who were decent towards me at the time. He was also a big personality. He was a Lance Bombardier and had been earmarked very early on in his career for great things. At the time of writing, he is a well-respected RSM and later Captain and I am happy to call him a friend.

After all of this excitement, and probably an awful lot of grovelling and apologies to the Greek Authorities, we set sail again and the destination this time was to be Egypt. It was roughly at this time that I noticed that my Army ID card was not in its normal place. I couldn't for the life of me remember what I had done with it and I searched everywhere I could think of without success. I knew that I would need my ID card if I wanted to get off the ship in the months ahead, so I went to see the Battery Clerk to tell him that I couldn't find it. If I needed to send off for a new one, I would need to do so through him, so I asked him what he thought I should do. I told him that I'd had it since we last set sail, so it was definitely on the ship somewhere and not in the hands of an unauthorised civilian, which is the main concern when an ID card is lost. I just needed to find it. I was worried about the BSM finding out and so I asked the Battery Clerk if it came to it and I had to apply for a new card, would the BSM have to find out? He said, "Yes, he will need to be told, but you have until the next time you want to be granted shore leave" – which was India. He would then just give me a temporary ID card that would cover me until my new one was sent out from the UK. India was not for several weeks so I had until then to find it, at which point I would need to tell the BSM. At this time, losing an ID card was a mandatory chargeable offence, although as long as it didn't keep happening it was a very minor thing. I know that later on, it ceased to be a chargeable offence and became simply an administrative affair as long as it didn't keep happening. Since joining the Army as a 16-year-old (nearly 10 years prior), I had never lost my ID before so I definitely was not a serial offender. But would this be taken into consideration with the BSM? I didn't want to find out – so I continued looking everywhere I could think of. I probably checked everywhere ten times over, but with no luck.

A couple of days later, we arrived in Port Said which is the gateway to the Suez Canal. This was a bustling port and although we did not dock alongside, we were still able to meet some of the locals. We were soon joined by lots of overladen little boats full of merchandise that the men on board were frantically attempting to sell to us whilst bobbing around in the choppy sea. One very insistent chap who was selling very old-fashioned leather jackets was shouting up in a heavily accented voice saying, "Eh mister, you buy these and you will look like a Michael Jackson!" Unfortunately for him, I don't think this was a compelling enough argument for us to buy his jackets! We also had to chase several locals off the ship who had clearly clambered on board to see what they could steal as an alternative way to make some money. A group of guys did go ashore and visited the Pyramids. Although I really wanted to go, I didn't because I didn't have my ID. But to be honest, even if I did have it I was feeling far too vulnerable at this point to risk not being made welcome by the others.

After leaving Port Said, we sailed down through Egypt along the Suez Canal, which is a fascinating voyage if you are experiencing it for the first time as I was. It's an amazing feat of engineering and certainly makes the sea voyage from the Mediterranean to the Red Sea an awful lot shorter by removing the need to sail around most of Africa to do it! Our next country to visit was Djibouti which is on the North East coast of Africa. This was a very depressing place as it is one of the poorest countries in the world. We only stayed for a short time but seized the opportunity to get ashore to go for a run as a group. I didn't need my ID for this as I was part of a squad of men. It was fascinating and troubling at the same time to see people living in such obvious poverty. Many people were just lying in the road, but it didn't look like some of them were resting because of the way they were lying, and where they were lying also didn't seem normal. I wondered if they were actually dead – but the locals didn't seem interested in these people lying in or by the road at all and so we just continued on in an uncomfortable silence. Visiting a country like this certainly makes you appreciate living in a first world country a lot more and is a reminder of what most of us take for granted at home.

The next phase involved sailing across the Arabian Sea to India. During the transit, which lasted several days, we got back into the routine of being at sea with jungle lectures and daily chores (as described earlier) including galley fatigues and guard shift. As a Bombardier I was allocated five other guys of Gunner and Lance Bombardier rank to be in charge of when it was our turn to complete guard and galley duties. This was straightforward enough, although one of the guys on my team, though a nice bloke, wasn't the brightest, which was a challenge at times! On one occasion, the guy who should have been relieved on Dolphin Watch got in touch with me saying he hadn't been replaced. Dolphin Watch was just a nickname for a duty requiring someone to watch from the stern of the ship to raise the alarm if anyone or thing fell overboard. I got on the ship's tannoy and called for the missing man to report to the military office to meet me. After several minutes, he hadn't arrived which got me a little worried – so I started searching the ship for him, but I couldn't find him anywhere. It occurred to me that he may not have done a Dolphin Watch yet and I tried to imagine what he may have thought when told to go on Dolphin Watch if he didn't actually know what it meant. One of the few places I hadn't been to yet was the focsle, which is located at the very front of the ship. In the Titanic movie, this is where Leonardo DiCaprio and Kate Winslet did the scene where she holds her arms out as if flying. Yes, you've probably guessed it: I found him there and when I asked him why, he told me he was looking for dolphins. I later had another issue relating to him, but it wasn't his fault. I walked past the galley on one occasion and I noticed that he was in the kitchen doing fatigues. My shift was on military office duties at this time, so I went to speak to him to ask what he was doing. I presumed that he was confused about what he should be doing but he informed me that he had been ordered to do it by a Bombardier who was head of the shift that was currently responsible for galley fatigues. This was a very odd thing for the Bombardier to do because he would know that my guy could not do both these duties at once, because over a 24-hour period there would be far too many overlaps and clashes. I asked my guy if he had told the Bombardier that he was currently on the guard shift and he said yes, he had. I asked him if he had done something wrong and he sincerely said no. Even if he had been made to do it as a punishment, the Bombardier would have known that he would need to speak to me about it first to both get my consent and to allow me to de-conflict my guard shift to enable my guy to do both. I could write out a long list of why it was wrong for him to detail my guy off in this way, but mainly, the Bombardier should have spoken to me first before doing it. Every single junior rank on board was allocated to a shift headed up by a JNCO, so anyone in his position would know that he should consult with a guy's immediate boss if he wanted to affect or alter his daily routine in any significant way. I thought about going to find him first to speak to him, but that would have been a weak response. I knew that every other Bombardier in my shoes would have stopped my guy from doing galley fatigues immediately, so that's exactly what I did. I could have gone to find the Bombardier to confront him about it, but rightly or wrongly I decided not to. About twenty minutes later, he came to see me very angry. "What the fuck are you doing overruling my decision," he said, to which I calmly replied, "it was not your decision to make, and if you wanted to use him in this way you should have spoken to me first. Why did you detail him off?" He did not have a reasonable reply, other than "Because I did, ok." To this day, I don't really know what he was thinking. Perhaps he just wanted to humiliate me into doing something that would undermine me, and maybe he banked on the fact that I would not stand up for myself (or my guy, for that matter). All I know is that I found the strength to look him firmly in the eye and say: "No, that's the end of the matter." He did not have an ounce of justification for his actions. So he wouldn't even have been able to get the BSM to come down on his side on the matter, so he backed down – although he was now seething with anger and resentment towards me, which would come to a head much later on in the tour.

Looking back on events like this now, with more knowledge of human behaviour, I think that he also felt very insecure. He was attempting to exert himself to feel better about himself and maybe gain more respect from others. Let's face it, I wasn't very popular, so if he 'put me in my place' as it were, maybe others would appreciate his action. If I needed any proof that he now had it in for me, I would soon find out. A couple of evenings later, I was in the rec space having a can of beer with some of the younger guys in the Bty. The more senior LBdrs and Bombardiers hadn't really accepted me yet, so I found myself socialising with more junior members. In most military units, the level of banter and taking the piss out of each other can be pretty extreme and I am relieved to say that it wasn't always directed towards me. The fact is that this particular Bombardier was also the butt of people's jokes from time to time and he didn't seem to cope with it that well, which as we all know only encourages people. He was a pretty normal looking guy, but I suppose if you scrutinised him very closely you could notice a couple of bumps on his forehead. The lads, who could be pretty merciless, decided that these bumps were like small horns, so he was given the nickname of Cowhead! I know he hated this, and to make matters worse, the lads would often make cow noises when he was around if they really wanted to wind him up.

He entered the rec space which was now full of guys who had had a few beers and, you guessed it, people started making cow noises really loudly. It turned into a competition as to who could make to loudest and most realistic cow noise! Just about everyone present including me was laughing loudly at the time, because to be honest, it was pretty funny. The only one who didn't find this funny was the Bombardier himself, who flew into a rage. After scanning the room, he saw where I was sitting and began throwing full unopened cans of beer at me with as much force as he could. I managed to avoid each can, as did the guys around me, which was lucky because it would definitely have hurt if a direct hit had taken place! I, as well as everyone else, knew hc was aiming at me and not the crowd because his eyes were focussed on me the whole time. After he had used up all the cans in his immediate vicinity, he angrily stomped out of the rec space. Under normal circumstances, I would not have stood for him targeting me like this and deliberately trying to hit me with the cans of beer, but again at the time my lack of self-confidence prevented me from reacting. So I just sat there and did nothing, hoping for the moment to pass so that people would not notice my weakness. I would stand up to him physically later on in the tour which actually then caused his aggressive behaviour towards me to stop. It's a shame that I didn't have the courage to do it sooner because it would have made my life so much easier, but that's just the way things were at the time with me.

In Trouble Again!

Our arrival in India was now drawing near and I had still not found my ID card. I was going to have to go and speak to the BSM which I was dreading, but there was no way around it unfortunately. It was at this time that I was summoned to go and see the BSM in the Military office. To my dismay he said, "The Battery Clerk informs me that you lost your ID card and tried to get him to get you a replacement without going through the proper channels or informing me." This was only partly correct but, without allowing me to speak, he informed me that I would go on Battery Commander's Orders to be charged for the loss of my ID card. The BSM acting this way towards me came as no surprise, but I was saddened that the Battery Clerk had chosen to portray what had happened to the BSM in such a way. Why did he not come and see me to say that I needed to tell the BSM myself or he would have to. I spoke to him about it afterwards but he didn't really want to speak about it and simply shrugged it off.

I found myself on BC's orders again for the second time inside of a year (it had never happened to me before 29 Cdo), which is not a nice experience because you are treated like a petty criminal. Once marched in to the BC's office, the BC tore into me saying things like: he expected much more from a Bdr and he was disgusted with my behaviour etc. Instead of the usual procedure of charging £50 for the loss, he decided to make it £100 in my case because of the accusation that I attempted to have the Bty Clerk bypass the system. Being treated like this is a bitter pill to swallow, especially when you are aware that the guys a couple of weeks earlier had fled a taxi without paying, with one assaulting a Greek Army Security Guard, after which they received no sanction apart from a rather stiff telling off. It was another stark reminder to me that I really had to watch my back, and I needed to be very careful indeed before trusting anyone again.

To add insult to injury, before we even got to India I found my ID card inside a book I had been reading. I remembered that I had used the card as a temporary bookmark, but unfortunately the book wasn't that interesting and it was a couple of weeks before I picked it up again. I gave my temporary card back but it did not change what had happened. We soon arrived in India and docked in a town called Cochin which is on the South Eastern coast to the south of

Goa. We were given a couple of days R&R here which allowed us to get ashore and spend some time in the local town. I resisted the temptation to stay on board and managed to latch on to a group of lads who were intent on finding a hotel to spend time away from the ship. I could tell my presence wasn't welcomed wholeheartedly by all, but I managed to tag along without anyone telling me to sod off. This was definitely progress because the more time I got to spend with the lads, the more I could actually be myself and allow them to get to know the real me and not the strange individual that had been imposed upon them.

I remember having a really good laugh when we all went out for a meal – unsurprisingly, to an Indian restaurant! As a bit of a challenge, we all ordered the hottest curries we dared to order which certainly caused a few red faces when the effects took hold. A lad called Mick rather unwisely announced at the table that he was immune to chilies and did not find them hot at all. About one second after making this audacious claim, a hand was in the air summoning the waiter to our table. The waiter was sent to get the hottest chili in the restaurant so that our confident friend could eat it and demonstrate his impressive ability to not be affected.

The waiter was a little concerned and suggested that it would not be a wise thing to do, but we insisted. The waiter reluctantly obeyed and retrieved a very innocent, tiny little chili from the kitchen and placed it in front of Mick who, after seeing the concern of the waiter, was not as confident as he had been. He decided that he couldn't back out now and grabbed the chilli, threw it into his mouth and began chewing vigorously. After a few seconds, he began to look reassured that he was in fact superior to this silly little bit of food and he looked around at his mates, nodding as if to say say, "I told you!" A few more seconds passed and then his expression began to change. His face went very quickly to a shade of red I have never seen before on a person. He began to suck in air frantically to cool his mouth and then grabbed his pint and started to drink it to see if that would help, but it didn't. Mick was now sweating profusely, his eyes and nose started to stream, and he had a panicked look of desperation on his beetroot-like face! It was like he had been poisoned and was going through the death throes that would inevitably lead to his untimely end. Not knowing what else to do, he jumped out of his seat and ran to the toilets deciding that the offending item was better out than in before it did any more damage! The whole thing was hilarious to watch, with poor old Mick not getting a great deal of sympathy from his mates as we were all roaring with laughter. I went after him to see if he was ok and I found him with his head under a cold tap of running water which had space underneath to allow buckets to be filled up. This allowed him to get his head fully underneath which is exactly where he stayed for some time until he began to feel a little better. Later, we all went to the hotel and I ended up sharing a twin room with Mick, which allowed us to get to know each other a little better and we got on ok: I was gradually making progress, which was great.

From India we sailed to Malaysia and docked in Kuala Lumpur, from where we went ashore to do some military training in the jungle. It was my first time of being in this environment and, although the high heat and humidity whilst performing arduous training made it quite a tough place to be, I really enjoyed it. Apart from the jungle being a vastly different environment to any other I had previously experienced, one man in each of our patrols also had to carry live ammunition as well as blank. To do this is virtually unheard of in the Army because of the risk of mixing up the ammo and the obvious danger that would entail. In Malaysia, however, the risk that we might encounter elephants in the jungle was deemed to be more of a threat, so we had to have live ammo at the ready in case we needed it to defend ourselves from an aggressive elephant! As well as infantry training, we did some survival training too. This involved living off the land and eating what you could catch, which wasn't much! The hardest part of survival training in the jungle was that we no longer had the use of our mosquito nets, and what made matters worse is the area we were made to use for this phase was near a river and quite boggy underfoot, which was an ideal environment for mosquitos. I am someone who attracts biting insects more than most and I was getting really badly bitten. I can remember the constant high-pitch hum that the mosquitos were making as they swarmed around us, unable to move away from the river, feasting on our blood. Every now and then, I would swat a mosquito and you could tell if it had already fed on one of us because there would be a large amount of blood appearing wherever the squashed 'mozzy' met its premature end. It was an uncomfortable couple of days spent in our improvised shelter and I reached the conclusion that if ever there was a creature that had no worthy purpose on this planet, mosquitos are that creature! I was glad that I had been taking my anti-malaria drugs and, fortunately for me, I didn't suffer any side effects form the tablets. Some of the guys did suffer side effects such as insomnia, dizziness, headaches and sickness from them and subsequently didn't take them. Some guys actually contracted malaria on Ocean Wave, which can come and go throughout someone's life, but if you are fortunate enough to live in a first world country it can be treated successfully and should not be too debilitating. After this phase was complete, we had some R&R in Kuala Lumpur which is when I started to feel quite ill. Although it was very hot, I was feeling very cold and shivery all the time. I was hoping that it would pass, but it lasted for several weeks. I didn't realise, but others noticed that I was getting really thin, so I was told to go and see the ship's doctor to get checked out. He took some blood samples which were sent off to be tested to see if my condition could be diagnosed. When the test results were in, the doctor summoned me to the sick bay to inform me that I had contracted some form of blood disorder. However, the exact condition could not be diagnosed, and therefore there was no actual treatment for me apart from not doing anything too strenuous or physically demanding. This was not good news for me because all I wanted was to prove myself as a worthy member of the Bty, and this was going to set me apart from the others even more. I did not intend to tell anyone what the doctor had said about curtailing any physical activity but unfortunately the doctor informed the BSM of his recommendations. The BSM called me into the 'Senior Rates Mess' which is the SNCO version of our rec space and informed me that I would not be going ashore to take part in the next serial of the exercise, which was a gunnery phase where we would revert back to being artillery soldiers, as opposed to infantry, and I would stay on board ship as a 'sickie'.

A sickie, as you can imagine, is a general term used to describe someone who is not fully fit and well. There is a certain stigma attached to sickies in any military unit, but to be a sickie in 29 Cdo was definitely not a good label to have, even if it was irrefutable that there was indeed something wrong with you. As the BSM spoke, my heart sank. In vain, I insisted that I was ok and I did not need to 'go on the sick' but he was not buying it. He said that I looked ill and his exact words were, "I'm not going to risk the possibility of you dropping dead ashore because I might get in the shit for going against doctor's orders."

As a soldier you do not need to be talked to softly by your superiors, but the way he chose to tell me why he was making his decision was particularly harsh I thought – even taking his resentment towards me into consideration. And so, I had to miss the next exercise in Malaysia and wait it out on board ship, which was not much fun. Once the exercise was complete, we left Malaysia, this time heading for Brunei, which is where we would be spending the next couple of months, and where the majority of our jungle training would take place. Our base in Brunei was a place called Sitang Camp which is also where the SAS go to for their jungle training. One of the lads from 29 Cdo was actually there at the time doing his jungle training whilst on his SAS selection course, which must have been a bit weird for him, being on the other side of the world and his former Regiment turning up in the same place.

Not far from camp was a theme park called Jerudong Park which had all of the usual things like rollercoasters and other scary rides. The Sultan of Brunei had the place built for his people to use and entry, as well as all the rides, was free. I am not sure if tourists had to pay to use the place, but as British soldiers we were allowed to use it for free which was pretty cool. One thing I found quite weird about Brunei was that without access to the Internet or digital radios, if you turned on any local bog-standard transistor radio you could tune in to Capital FM. Apparently, the Sultan enjoyed Capital FM when spending time in London and so paid to have the station re-broadcast in Brunei.

Coming to Blows

I was now feeling and looking a lot better, so I was allowed to take part in the military training. Although I really enjoyed the Infantry training and time spent in 'the trees,' I was keen to take part in the artillery exercises because this is where I knew I could impress with all of the gunnery knowledge I had attained at Larkhill, due to all of the live firing I had done on Salisbury Plain. Although there was always an underlying tension with my second-in-command on my gun detachment, he was always professional and tried his best whenever we were on exercise. The guy I had operating the sights on the gun was called Kel and he was a very keen and intelligent guy who would go on to be one of the youngest Sergeant Majors in the Artillery and became what was called a "flyer", meaning that he was someone who was flying through the ranks. He and I would later go on to be good friends although there was definitely some tension between us in the early days.

One of the lads on my gun who I liked a lot from the minute I met him was a Welsh lad called Welly. I taught him how to sing *American Pie*, which was hilarious because he would always get the words mixed up and his singing was terrible! As a gun detachment we were pretty formidable, and I began to get complimented on how good we were as a team. It felt good to finally get some positive recognition. I do remember one occasion when doing my job to the best of my ability did invite some negativity from my peers – in particular, one of the other gun number ones. There is a command called 'check firing' given from the Command Post (CP) to the Guns – and until the command "Cancel check firing" is given, you cannot fire, even if the CP gives you the order to fire. If they order you to fire but have not cancelled check firing, you must ask them to cancel check firing first. I got flak from this Gun's number one who was a well-respected member of the Bty because the command post gave the order to the guns to fire but had not cancelled a 'check firing' given earlier.

One of the other Guns in the Battery fired, but I asked the CP to cancel check firing first. They cancelled check firing and I then fired. This inevitably made the guy who had already fired look bad. I was told I should have just fired anyway because it was obvious that the CP had just forgotten to cancel check firing. I agreed that it was extremely likely that the CP had just forgotten. However, the culture I had become used to in 34 Bty was one of technical gunnery. It was perfectly normal for a gun number one to do what I did – even if it embarrassed someone else – because it was considered that doing things by the rule book was more important than someone else's blushes. In fact, when I was an inexperienced number one myself, I was the one who fired in this type of situation when I shouldn't have a few times and was left feeling embarrassed, but I soon learnt and didn't do it again.

It was assumed that I had only done it on this occasion to make one of my fellow number ones look bad, so unfortunately this caused negativity towards me again. If I had just fired, there would have been no animosity generated and no one would have assumed I was trying to upstage a fellow number one. With hindsight, whilst trying to get accepted in the Bty that might have been the better option. I did go and apologise to the number one in question later on and he told me not to worry and to forget about it. But unfortunately others were not so willing to let it go.

In between being on exercise, we would often have what's called a Bty Smoker, which is basically our evening meal in the form of a BBQ and a few cans of beer. After one such smoker, the tension between Kel and myself came to a head. He had had a few too many beers and the banter which can normally be pretty harsh started to get a little edgy. Normally a Gunner, even with beer involved, would not be too disrespectful towards a Bombardier, but he was definitely not holding back at this point. He said something about my family and so I returned the same type of sentiment to a member of his family. At this point Kel leaped to his feet and stood directly in front of where I was sitting on a chair, and without any warning began to rain punches down onto the top of my head.

I can remember trying to get up, but he was standing in my way and whilst he was beating down on me, I found it impossible to move. All I could do was to cover up as best I could and wait for the punches to stop. This went on for about five to ten seconds which was enough time for me to receive multiple punches to the head. I don't know if anyone pulled him off or if he stopped when he was ready. All I know is that when the blows ceased coming, I removed my hands and raised my head again to see him standing a few feet away, breathing heavily from his exertion and staring at me still full of anger and aggression. I was still in a state of shock over what had just happened, but there was no way I was going to let it go and accept the beating I had just taken. I stood up calmly and said, "Ok Kel, now let's you and I go outside on the grass and have a fair fight." We walked out on to the grass and the other lads who were around at the time followed. I led the way and when I had reached a suitable spot, I turned around and said, "Ok let's go." I don't remember exactly how the fight went but I do know one thing that my dad always impressed upon me from a young age which was, "If you get into a fight you really have to make your first punch count because that might be the only clean punch you get." I know that I got a really good clean initial punch in on him and his eye began to swell immediately.

I do not remember getting hit again in this scuffle and we ended up grappling on the floor until the fight was broken up by some passers-by. We agreed to call a truce and with the excitement now over, it seemed a good enough time to get a shower and get to bed. In the morning, my head above the hairline was feeling really sore and I had many lumps and bumps. The only visible injury Kel had was a black eye, and this was inevitably going to generate questions from the hierarchy in the Bty. A fight between us would make us both look bad and so we wanted to try to hide it if we could. Kel and I decided to concoct a story which was that one of the lads had thrown a piece of kit from the back of our gun-towing vehicle and it had accidentally hit him in the face causing his black eye. The BSM approached us whilst we were working on our gun and asked how he had got the black eye and we gave him our story. It was very obvious that he did not believe a word of it, but he decided not to pursue it any further, which was a relief.

I think this fight with Kel was a seminal moment for me because he was definitely no push-over and people could now see that I was prepared to defend myself physically if necessary, and this helped me gain respect. I still had a long way to go, but again this was progress. A little later on in the tour, Kel had a similar altercation with a sergeant, and the sergeant ended up with quite a nasty black eye. They had both been drinking and Kel was defending one of his mates, as apparently the sergeant was being aggressive towards him. When I heard about this, it actually made me feel a lot better about his previous aggression towards me, because it didn't single me out as different and it suggested it was more about him and how he dealt with others. The incident between him and the sergeant also got brushed under the carpet because the sergeant was not blameless and it would have negatively impacted on them both if it had been taken any further.

It was another reminder to me though of how some guys could get away with murder if they were liked and respected by the chain of command. I know if I had done anything similar whilst under the command of the BSM I would have had the book thrown at me, and it would have cost me a lot of money and would probably have got me demoted as well. The two instances where I was charged and fined for being late for parade (or not, as was the case) and misplacing my ID card were certainly testament to that. It reinforced to me that I would have to really keep my nose clean if I was to survive this period in 29 Cdo without falling foul of the BSM or anyone else who did not wish me well.

I am glad to say that things were starting to improve for the better. I was gaining respect for my ability as a gun number one and as my self-confidence began to improve, I was starting to make friends. I wasn't experiencing too much in the way of friction from anyone in particular at that time.

Meanwhile Back Home

The exercise was now a few months in and it felt weird being away from Siân for such a long time. I was however able to keep in regular contact and she seemed very happy living with my mum and Terry, who had now moved to Swansea. My sister Lisa, who also lives in Swansea with my nephew Callum (who is two years younger than Siân) has also played a big part in Siân's life. Siân and Callum grew up more like brother and sister during her early years. My brother Johnny also moved to live in Swansea and so Siân had lots of my family around her which was reassuring to me. The reason so many of my immediate family were moving there seemed to be down to my dad.

Dad and Tommo had sold Barking Football Social Club and gone their separate ways in business, but remained good friends. Dad decided to remain in the pub trade because, although it was hard work, he had made good money. So he looked to see what else the breweries were offering as available. With his new partner Karen, he moved to a town in South Wales called Maesteg where he and another ex-Army friend ran the Four Sevens Country Club. Dad's friend had been an Officer in 29 Cdo whilst Dad was in the Regiment. At one time he was the Officer in Command of the Pre-Cdo Course and my dad was his Sergeant. They remained friends afterwards and now decided to go into business together. This did not work out though, unfortunately, and so they decided to go their separate ways. Via the brewery my dad spotted another opportunity, this time in Swansea. He bought the Morriston Sport and Social Club which, like Barking, also became a great success.

Dad's business partner Steve would eventually buy my dad out of the club completely and he still owns it to this day. Dad and Karen went on to have four children: Alex, Lauren, Emma and Sarah.

Mum and Terry's decision to go to Swansea is again down to my dad's involvement in property. My mum and dad have always remained on good terms since their divorce and Dad and Terry got on really well. Dad and Terry had a lot in common due to the fact that Terry had spent most of his working life as a Royal Marine and, at the time, Terry was working as a Captain with a TA Regiment of the Royal Green Jackets working Monday to Friday in London. Terry sold his house in Plymouth and he and my mum pooled their money to have a detached house built in Swansea using my dad's contacts in the building trade. Mum and Terry rented a house from my dad whilst the house was built and then moved in with Siân. So the main reason that so many of my family have lived or are living in Swansea is down to my dad's influence.

With so many of my family members around Siân, it certainly made this time in my life a lot easier to cope with. It was mainly my mum and Terry who were providing the parental support that a child needs, whilst I contributed financially. Although I was away for a long time on this occasion, I made sure I saw Siân as much as possible on leave and at weekends whilst she was living in Swansea. I certainly leaned on my family for help and support during the next few years and, looking back, I don't know if the right thing to do would have been to have left the Army then – and that is something I wrestle with to this day.

One of the issues I was battling was that I had no idea what I could do outside of the Army. If a serviceman is given no choice but to leave, he will invariably find something to do. But the reality is that you can become indoctrinated in the Army, especially if you have also grown up inside the Army and been to boarding school. My self-confidence was still not good at this time, so thoughts of a different career scared me too much. So I chose to stay in – at least for the time being. I decided that I would continue to review the situation and that if Siân seemed happy and also if my mum was ok with the situation, I would keep things as they were for the time being.

The Tour Continues

After the Brunei phase was complete, we sailed to the Philippines to conduct some training there. But, for whatever reason, that was cancelled and so we were given some R&R. A group of us got a flight to Manila and stayed in a hotel there for a few days. I had a really good time and I was starting to feel happy and more confident and I was making friends. After the Philippines, we sailed to Singapore which is where the ship would stay during the main R&R phase. Most of the guys decided to go to Thailand from here, although a group of us decided to go to Bali instead because it is somewhere many Australians go to party, so it seemed like the ideal place to visit.

I am glad we did because I had a really great time in Bali and it's also the time that I struck up a good friendship with a lad called Mark, also known as Sarse. Apparently, it has something to do with aftershave that he wore once that smelled a bit like Sarson's vinegar. For some reason this nickname seemed to stick, and twenty years later he is still called Sarse! He and I realised that we had a fair bit in common in that we had both been squaddie brats and been to boarding school. We realised that we shared a similar sense of humour and we could make each other laugh a lot.

Bali was great, but it unfortunately had a problem with pickpockets and thieves at the time. Many of these thieves were gangs of kids who operated in packs. They would often gather in a place that forced you to walk through them. Human nature causes you to put your hand over where your wallet or valuable item is on you person. Unfortunately, this tells them exactly where they need to target and when they swarm around you, they will do anything to get you to move your hand from where you are protecting your stuff. A couple of them might grab your bag and half-heartedly try to wrestle it away from you. When you use both hands to grab the bag to stop them getting it, they nab your wallet, which you had already identified as your most valuable asset. If you feel it being taken and grab the kid in question, they are very fast and the wallet will already be in the hands of another kid and they will be away. If you try to hold on to the kid for any length of time, the kid will scream as if you are attacking him and the men will appear aggressively from the shadows. You inevitably will let go of the child and hold your hands up as if to say, "I wasn't hurting him," and the child will then disappear along with the men. It is at this point you realise it was all a military-style tried and tested operation.

I saw this happen a couple of times to other tourists and it is all over in seconds. As a group we decided to only go out with relatively small amounts of cash kept loose and spread around different pockets to throw them off, which worked well. At the end of an evening, I was less aware of danger and I had my watch stolen off my wrist by a gang of kids. It was a pretty decent Citizen diver's watch that my friend Gary had sold to me a couple of years earlier. I loved my watch and the really annoying thing was that whenever I forgot and looked at my wrist to check the time, I would be reminded of the disappointment of losing it over and over again which was a real pain! I don't know if I am the unluckiest man in the world but unlikely as it may seem, I also managed to get robbed by a policeman whilst in Bali!

Up until then, all we had done was visit bars in the town of Kuta, so I decided to hire a moped for the day so I could explore the island a bit more. I didn't venture too far from the town as I didn't want to get lost, but I got to see a little bit more of the nearby scenery and countryside at least. Just before arriving back at the bike hire shop, a policeman who was standing on the pavement waved at me to stop on a slow-moving stretch of road. I duly stopped and he began to speak to me in English. He informed me that I had passed through a no entry sign and I would need to show him my ID and driver's licence. I showed him my Army ID and my licence and after examining both, I noted that he did not immediately give them back. I looked back in the direction I had just been for the no entry sign, but I could not see one. I asked him where it was and he pointed, but I said I still could not see it. He then walked over and pointed to a no entry sign that was completely obscured by the leaves of a bushy tree. I complained that it was impossible to see the sign, but he simply shrugged and changed the subject. He said he would have to confiscate my ID and licence and I would have to appear in court at a later date. I would be able to argue about the sign not being visible then. He said he would issue me with a receipt for my documents and I would get them back after the court date in a couple of weeks.

Clearly, it was impossible for me to either wait until the court date or return to Bali for it, which is what I told him. He said if I paid a fine now, I would not need to go to court and the fine was the equivalent of £50. The penny dropped that he was simply extorting money from me and this was probably the perfect spot right by the obscured sign to collar unsuspecting tourists in cars and on bikes. I decided that it would be a risky strategy to refuse to pay anything as he could maybe arrest me on a trumped-up charge, so I decided to play along. I had become used to bartering in this part of the world, so I complained at the amount and said I only had the equivalent of £30 on me. (I had more than this but it was in different pockets and I knew which one the £30 was in.) He suggested that I could give him my Ray-Ban sunglasses instead, but these were worth a lot more than that and I reacted strongly against this suggestion. There is clearly only so far someone in his position can take this scam – which was basically 'I will let you go on your way for a sum of money.' He was able to gauge exactly how much money to play for depending on how gullible or wealthy his victim was. He decided to accept the £30 which I was able to take out of my pocket without having to take it from a larger amount. I was relieved that I remembered successfully which pocket the £30 was in and didn't pull out a larger stash of cash. I gave him the money in exchange for my ID and licence and I was on my way. When I told the lads what had happened to me, they speculated that maybe he had actually found it necessary to fine me because of the ridiculous outfit I was wearing. I had decided to go out that day in white shorts and a white t shirt with white trainers and unfortunately the helmet I was given was also white. So, on reflection, they did have a point – I did look ridiculous and probably deserved to be fined, at least by the fashion police!

After a memorable time in Bali, we flew back to Singapore and met up with the rest of the Battery to hear of the many exploits that took place in Thailand, most of which I am unable to share! I was speaking to one of the lads about watches and he said that the diver's watch that he had paid £100 for in Singapore a couple of weeks before had rusted up after swimming in the pool in Thailand. I said his watch didn't sound like a genuine diver's watch and asked him where he got it from. He said the nearby market. So I told him that he had been ripped off and that he should go back to the stall and ask for his money back. He returned some hours later and said that the man would not give his money back, but it was ok because he had taken down his home address and would send the watch off to the manufacturer and get it repaired or replaced and then sent to him in Britain. With a sigh, I explained to him that the guy was not going to get the watch repaired because the watch was a fake and that he would be waiting a long time for a shiny new watch to arrive in the post from Singapore! I wanted to help him get his money back, so I went to see the Royal Marine Police officer on board the ship and I explained what had happened and asked if he would try to convince the trader to return the money. I suggested that he could threaten to return with the local civilian police if he didn't cooperate. The RMP guy agreed to help and dressed in uniform he accompanied my friend to where the market trader was. He was a happy man when he came back on board because the ploy worked and he got his money back!

Once we were all safely back on board, we sailed towards Hong Kong for the takeover event scheduled for July 1, 1997. The takeover went without incident and thankfully we were not required to do anything to help. The only excitement we had at this time was being buzzed at low level by a Chinese recognisance plane but that was it. We then sailed back to Singapore which is where we would say goodbye to our ship *Sir Geraint* as we were now due to fly to South Africa for the final six weeks of the tour.

I had decided that the only way I was going to be able to put my watch being stolen behind me was to replace it with as close a model as I could find. I decided not to chance my arm in the market in Singapore. Instead, I waited until I was in the duty-free area in the airport. The make of watch was a Citizen and, luckily, I found the exact make and model there which I purchased with my credit card for about £400. This was July 1997 and I was still wearing it after several operational tours in 2018, so If anyone who works for Citizen reads this book, let me know if you would like a testimonial about the quality of your watches!

From Singapore we flew to a place called Bloemfontein, which is in central South Africa, and we were allowed to travel in civilian clothes for the journey. Bearing in mind we had just spent over five months in the Far East, we were very accustomed to being in shorts and T-shirts whenever in civvies, and so that's what we were wearing when we arrived in Africa. What we were not aware of was that Bloemfontein was over 4.5 thousand feet above sea level and was definitely not as warm as we were expecting! In fact, I reckon the temperature at the time was below 10 degrees C. We were not reunited with our bags for over an hour and we were made to wait in an unheated hangar in the meantime and it was bloody freezing! It's a mistake I certainly won't make again: assuming that a country is hot and not bothering to check out the altitude, which significantly drops the average temperature of a place!

Once we got our bags, we got properly dressed and awaited the transport to take us to the nearby training area where we would conduct military training with the South African Army. After this phase, we did some more jungle training before being allowed some R&R, after which we would return to the UK. Many of the guys decided to go to Capetown, but I opted for Durban. South Africa was quite a surreal place to be not long after the end of Apartheid. At night-time, the sound of gunfire was common which is quite an odd thing to experience. Along the beaches of Durban there was a heavy armed police presence because, according to the locals I spoke to, there was a lot of crime and violence to be dealt with and tourists needed to be protected. On one occasion, a few of us accepted a lift from a local from one bar to another. But the female driver did not stop at any red lights; she simply slowed down to check nothing was coming. Apparently, this was because armed robbers would often hijack less aware people who made the mistake of stopping at a red light! A couple of the lads had acquired high-powered laser pointers in the Far East (this was before they became common), and decided it would be hilarious to see people's reactions when they noticed what could easily be mistaken as a laser from a sniper rifle trained upon them. After a while the lads with the lasers decided they had better stop their mischievous behaviour before they were either shot or arrested!

Back in the Fray

The animosity from the Bombardier who had detailed my guy off whilst on board ship reappeared at this point, although I honestly do not know what I had done to upset him. Although we were all staying at different hotels, there was a particular bar on the beach where we would all gather in the evenings. I thought it was just clumsiness at first, but he kept bumping into me and knocking me with his arm or elbow. Once I realised it was deliberate, at first I tried to ignore it, but he was clearly trying to provoke a reaction. Eventually, I had had enough, so I put my drink down and said, "Ok, let's go outside and settle this."

The bar was set by the beach on stilts and there was an outside balcony where people could also drink. From the balcony there was a suspended walkway that bridged the gap from the upstairs to the beach promenade. This walkway which was blocked off at the far end seemed as good a place as any for us to have the fight, which seemed likely at this point. So I led the way along the walkway to about the half-way point where I stopped and turned to face him. It was now completely up to him if we had a fight. I was willing to talk, argue or fight – it didn't matter to me. All I knew is that I wasn't willing to put up with the way he was acting any longer. It seemed that he was quite keen to have a fight – so that's exactly what happened. I can't claim to have got a really good initial punch in, but I was definitely landing blows and not receiving any. There was a lot of stored-up anger and frustration in me at this point: I was ready to really unload on him and it felt like he was only just keeping me at bay. But not for long! It was at this point that one of the other bombardiers came over and pulled us apart. He was a well-respected member of the Battery and also had a reputation for being a hard man, so this was definitely a significant intervention.

With only one man between us, we were still intent on continuing the fight. Punches were still being thrown, which started to annoy him a little, and he announced quite clearly that unless we both stopped fighting that he was going to join in. This got our attention because neither of us wanted to get into a fight with him, so we stopped at that point. I must admit that I was frustrated he had stopped the fight because I was feeling very confident at that point and, as far as I was concerned, my opponent was really going to get it. In hindsight, he definitely did me a favour. It would not have done either of us any good to get arrested, or to be visibly hurt when we would soon re-join the rest of the Bty, and the obvious questions would be asked by the BSM. It still felt like unfinished business between us, but I was now in more of a conciliatory frame of mind. I just wanted to know what it was about me that was winding him up so much.

The next evening, we both ended up in the same nightclub away from the beach bar. I approached in a very calm manner in order to have a chat, but at this point he started to act in a very odd way. He began to make a scene, shouting and waving his arms around and telling me to fuck off and leave him alone. I was genuinely confused and held my hands wide in a placating way and asked him what he was doing. I might be wrong but as I write this, I am very suspicious that he may have set me up at this point. Within seconds, a couple of bouncers came over to me and told me I would have to leave the club. This was also strange because I wasn't fighting or shouting or acting aggressively towards anyone at all – and even if I was, it would surely take a lot longer for bouncers to appear in what was a very large place. I now strongly suspect that after seeing me in the club, he must have spoken to the bouncers and said that I might attack him and to keep an eye on things. So, when he started shouting, they must have assumed I was picking on him in some way and told me to leave. I was really confused and frustrated at this point because I have never been thrown out of a place before. I am not someone who starts fights or causes trouble.

Once outside of the club, I could either have gone back to my hotel or waited for him there. I still wanted to speak to him and ask what was going on because the whole thing between us was ridiculous. To date he had interfered with my shift, thrown beer cans at me in the rec space, banged into me several times in the bar which led to us fighting the night before, and now due to some bizarre antics in the night club he had succeeded in getting me thrown out. I now had a strong desire not to bury my head in the sand any longer, but to confront it head on and hopefully put an end to it. I waited outside on my own for about an hour before he came outside with some of the others. When he saw me, I made sure that I acted in a non-aggressive manner and I said, "Can I please just have a chat with you, I don't want to have a fight, I just want to talk." I was relieved that he accepted and didn't cause a fuss and he came over to indeed talk. We spoke for a few minutes but he didn't really explain to me what it was that I was doing that was winding him up so much. I don't know whether he just couldn't articulate it very well or if he actually knew himself what the problem was, but ultimately, he agreed to call a truce and to put what had happened behind us and try to get along from now on. I am very happy to say that we did not clash with each other again.

This was now virtually the end of Exercise Ocean Wave and it had been a rollercoaster of high and low emotions. Looking back, it was like a baptism of fire in 29 Cdo Regiment because I felt it was a sink or swim situation in many ways. I felt like I was drowning on so many occasions and it certainly felt at times like I was never going to make it through. I think that the eight months away with 8 Bty was exactly what was required for me at that point – because without it, I would have continued to be isolated from the rest of the Regiment; I would not have been able to forge any real friendships or fight for my place and acceptance in the Bty. I think that before and during the tour, I was thought of as that strange crap hat (he's got his green beret but he still isn't really one of us) who doesn't really talk to people. But I finished it as Pony who's a good gun number one, likes a drink and a laugh, is physically fit, and can stick up for himself if he has to. That was a much nicer place to be than the place I was in before, and I felt confident that I would never be going back there again. I now felt optimistic about my future in 29 Cdo which felt great!

Although I seemed to have won over the lads in the Battery, I knew that the BSM was another kettle of fish entirely. The good news for any soldier is that if you have a boss who doesn't like you, he or she will only be in place for two to three years before they move on to either a promotion or a sideways position. I therefore knew that I simply had to wait it out. If I didn't manage to win him over, he would not be in a position of power over me for too much longer.

Family First

As soon as I got back to the UK, I went to Swansea to spend time there with Siân and the family. Siân, now four years old, was naturally excited to see me and it was great to be able to spend some prolonged quality time with her. Mum and Terry said it was good to have me back in the UK again, so that I could be around more which would give them a break from time to time.

After a few weeks on leave I went back to work and I was informed that the BSM had selected me to go back to Brunei to go on a jungle warfare instructors' course. This was not good news for me because it would involve being away for a long time again just after coming back from an eight-month trip. Surely the BSM knew my circumstances with Siân and the need for me to be around as much as possible. It caused me a real dilemma because I knew that it would look bad for me to ask not to go for compassionate reasons, and it would not be a good career move to do that, but it would be completely unfair on Mum, Terry and Siân for me to go away again for a long time so soon. I hated doing it so I went to see the BSM and asked for him to send someone else because of the impact it would have on my family situation. I had already spoken to one of the guys who I knew really wanted to go on the course and he was willing to volunteer if the BSM agreed to send someone else instead of me. The BSM was not very happy with me but reluctantly agreed to allow the other guy to go instead, which was a relief, but I knew it wasn't a good career move. Now that I felt more accepted in the Regiment, I naturally wondered how long it might take me to get to my next promotion which was sergeant. I did not expect to get promoted whilst the BSM was in place, so I looked forward to the following year when he was due to move on. In the meantime I decided just to keep my head down and get on with it as best I could. Apart from quite short exercises lasting less than a couple of weeks, I was able to get home to Swansea most weekends for the rest of that year.

First Sign of Injury

One of these exercises was mountain training that is often done prior to a Norway deployment. 3 Commando Brigade are the designated cold weather specialists and so, almost every year, 29 Cdo will deploy there to keep up to speed with operating in Arctic conditions. The main activity on mountain training, unsurprisingly, is navigating on foot in mountainous areas, although Royal Marine instructors would often teach rope-work such as abseiling and river crossings. Another activity was the death slide which is used to get a body of men down a cliff quickly. The rope is fastened at the top of the cliff and away from the base which creates a diagonal roughly 45-degree incline from top to bottom. First you place your hand through a loop on a short, thick piece of rope. You then raise the short rope above the descending rope and then place your hand through the loop at the other end of the short rope. You are now able to slide down the descending rope with only the centre of the short rope in contact with the descending rope. For guys that are afraid of heights this can be a bit of a scary thing to do, but I really enjoy things like this and so I was looking forward to my turn. Once I was 'hooked on' properly, the instructor at the top allowed me to start my descent. Although I am quite a large bloke there are lots of guys heavier than me and so it was strange why I picked up so much speed on my way down the rope. There were a couple of instructors at the bottom of the rope whose job it was to act as brake men, to slow you down before you make contact with the ground. They didn't slow me down much at all and I remember seeing them both become airborne once my momentum took hold as they followed after me. I landed with my feet and knees together as we had been taught but I hit the ground too hard for this to prevent injury. I immediately felt a sharp pain in my right ankle which gave way, causing me to collapse to the deck. My ankle began to swell up immediately but luckily nothing was broken. Fortunately, this was the last serial of the day and so I limped off to the transport which would take us back to camp. The next day we were due to go up into the mountains with Bergans on our backs and I knew my ankle would need to get a lot better overnight if I was going to be able to take part. I was dreading the scenario of the BSM finding out that I would not be taking part in the training even if he learnt I had been injured, because I knew he would not sympathise at all. In the morning my limp was just as bad, so I went to see one of the medics who I knew quite well as we were in the Regimental cross-country team together and completed the Commando course at the same time. I asked him to try and tape me up because this can help a lot with this type of injury. When he saw my ankle, which was black and blue and badly swollen, he said he was not prepared to tape me up, and he could not allow me to go up into the hills carrying this injury. I knew he was right because even if I was able to begin the 'yomp', if I was later unable to continue on foot, I would become a liability to myself and others which would be a significant safety risk. I asked him if he would go and inform the BSM that I had asked to be taped up in order to take part because I really didn't want to see him. I could imagine the look of disapproval on his face. Not long after, the BSM came to the sick bay to speak to me and, as I had predicted, he was not happy. He actually accused me of being a malingerer and said that I had also pulled a 'sickie' on Ocean Wave (when I missed one of the Malaysia exercises) and I was now getting a reputation as a malingerer. Without allowing me to respond to these accusations, he then left the sickbay. Even though I knew he had a low opinion of me, I was gobsmacked at what he said. He was the one who summoned me on board ship and told me he was not going to allow me to go ashore until I was better because he didn't want to get into any trouble if I dropped dead. It was just so bizarre how he chose to behave towards me, but all I could do was wait for the day he was no longer my boss, because that would be a great day for me! Unfortunately for me, the following year saw the BSM promoted to Regimental Sergeant Major (RSM) of 29 Cdo Regt. I was gutted by this news because as the RSM he would still have a major influence on who would be promoted to Sergeant within the Regiment as a whole. One consolation was that as the RSM I wouldn't really have much contact with him any more, whereas previously it had been very regular, so I was at least happy about that.

Army and Sport

29 Cdo is a regiment that performs well against the rest of the Army at most sports, but it did not have a Tug of War team. I asked my new BSM, who I had a good relationship with, if he would ask the Battery Commander to ask the CO if I could start up a Regimental team. Once the word spread, a SNCO Staff Sergeant (SSgt) McLoughlin offered to help out as the ToW officer. This was useful to have when dealing with officers or SNCOs from inside and outside of the Regiment and when trying to organise anything that needed to be done for the team other than the coaching itself. Permission was granted and so I went about asking for any willing volunteers from the Plymouth-based batteries. A lad called Stevo who had been on the tug of war team with me in 14 Regiment had also come to 29 Cdo and he was eager to take part, which was great for me because we were friends and he was already an accomplished 'puller'. In fact, Stevo was in the ToW team when he was in Junior Leaders and that team was so good that it went on to represent Britain at ToW internationally at the under-18 level.

Another lad that I had become good friends with since Ocean Wave was Daz. We found that we also had a lot in common as his dad had also served in 29 Cdo at the same time as my dad, and so we shared a very similar upbringing. It just so happened that Daz had also been in the same ToW team as Stevo when he was at Junior Leaders, so I already had two really good guys to take part. I was delighted with the fact that several other good blokes from the Regiment decided to join the team with me as the coach, which was testament to how far I had come since the start of my time in the Regiment. One of the guys Kel, who I had fought with previously, was on the team but we now got on really well, as I did with another guy called Will. Both he and Will were really good pullers and got to a good standard very quickly. As a team, we started off doing very well in Army competitions despite a relative lack of experience.

After only a few weeks training we came third in the UK land forces competition, which is basically open to any Army, Navy or RAF UK-based unit. I can remember that the 14 Regt team I was in took a lot longer to get to this standard, so I was getting pretty excited about what we could go on to achieve.

The blue-ribbon event in the Military ToW calendar each year is the Highland Games in Scotland which takes place in early September in Braemar, the final of which is watched by the Queen and other members of the Royal Family. In order to prepare properly for the Games, you need to have several weeks of good training leading up to it. The only issue with that is the fact that summer leave for most military units takes place in August. So, in order to properly prepare, a ToW needs to take their summer leave early to then return and train as a team for the remaining weeks leading to the competition. This takes a significant level of buy-in from the Regiment. I had twelve guys on the team which caused an amount of juggling of commitments to be done by the guys' respective Battery to be able to accommodate this. The only way this can happen is if the CO gives his full support and commands each Battery to cooperate and facilitate the different leave requirements. ToW was not a recognised Regimental sport like rugby or football is, so I was pleasantly surprised that my request for this was granted.

We all subsequently took our leave early and then returned to camp to commence training just as everyone else was going on their leave. It was at this point that I was informed that two of my best pullers had dropped out of the team, which was a really disappointing development because I was definitely planning on picking them for the final eight that would pull in Braemar. They were not there for me to ask, so I was completely in the dark about what had happened and why they had pulled out. SSgt McLoughlin arrived and once I told him he said he would go and speak to their respective BSMs to ask what had happened. I got on with training the rest of the team, but before the end I was interrupted by a lad who said I had to go and see the RSM.

I told the guys I would be back asap and so, a little confused and apprehensively, I went to RHQ and received another very odd outburst from him. He told me to stop complaining about the fact that the guys were off the team and accept it. He then stated that both, although junior in rank to me, would overtake me and be Sergeant Majors, maybe directly in charge of me in the future, and because I would never get to that rank, I should be careful not to upset them if I knew what was good for me! A little bit shocked, I simply said, "Ok, Sir." What else could I do? I returned to continue training the remaining guys on the team. When I eventually did get to speak to them both, they basically said that they just didn't want to do ToW any more and their respective batteries wanted them back to normal work, so instead of training with us they got to go on leave again with the rest of the Regiment.

Although I was disappointed, I felt no urge to fall out with them. If they were no longer committed, then so be it. I am still friends with them both to this day. The RSM was also correct about them both being Sergeant Majors in the future, but I am very pleased to say that neither of them overtook me during my career because I managed to get back on track once he was no longer in my chain of command. I am sure if he had been in control of my career indefinitely they would have done, but fortunately for me, after he finished his tour as RSM I would never serve in the same Regiment as him again.

The team did its best at Braemar but we only beat a few teams in the end and didn't do as well as we had done earlier in the year. It was a fantastic experience though and I am very proud to say that I was the coach of the Regimental team at the time. Sadly, a few years later (after leaving the army), Stevo tragically died of cancer in his mid-thirties and he is sorely missed. RIP Stevo.

With this experience now behind me, I returned to normal work which I was actually starting to enjoy. I had made some good friends and I was gaining respect from my peers and my superiors. It was in this environment that I was able to make myself eligible for promotion to Sergeant. The RSM was coming to the end of his tenure in the Regiment and although I doubt he supported my promotion, I know I had the support of my own BSM and Battery Commander now. Ultimately, this was enough to get me over the line and I was informed in 2000 that I would soon be promoted. I had been a Bombardier for over seven years which was quite unusual to be in that rank for so long, and so in my opinion going to 29 Cdo slowed down my career progression considerably, and I honestly believe that it was the RSM who had a large part to play in that. Now, in a strange way, I sort of sympathise with him for having such a low opinion of me because he never saw me operating anywhere near my potential because of the low self-esteem I struggled with during my time under his command. The reality, however, is that his unprofessional and vindictive behaviour towards me contributed to this, and he even created a culture in 8 Battery whereby it was ok to disrespect me and put me down. In many ways, despite our differences, the BSM was a good and capable soldier. It's a shame that things went wrong between us and that he seemed to have it in for me, though, as I say, I understand (to an extent) his feelings.

Even as I write this, I am telling myself that I should have been stronger, that I should have stood up for myself sooner and better, that ultimately it was me who let him and others affect my state of mind so much. But unfortunately, I can't go back in time and tackle it with the self-confidence and self-belief that I now have. I just have to accept the past and learn from it. I have to admit that I am embarrassed to write about how vulnerable and open to being bullied I was during that time in my life. But I hope that by writing about it I might give hope to someone else who may be experiencing similar issues, either as a child or an adult, because you can get through it.

Messed Up Mess Dress

In the military, we are told in advance when being promoted to Sergeant, as it gives us the chance to get our Mess Dress made to measure. This is a uniform that is worn at functions in the Sergeants' Mess and is the military equivalent to a tuxedo. A little controversially, at the time of writing, mess dress isn't paid for or provided by the Army. So you need to go to military tailors, that you will find in most garrison towns, who provide this service and pay several hundred pounds for it. Another guy who was going to be promoted at the same time as me was Eddie. We both got our mess dress ordered from the local tailors but, unfortunately, they made a mistake and cut it from the wrong cloth. The correct colour of Royal Artillery mess dress is 'Midnight Blue', but they made ours from a lighter blue cloth, although neither of us noticed at the time because we weren't familiar enough with what the mess dress should have looked like. Eddie attended a mess function before me and had it pointed out to him, so he informed me that mine was probably wrong as well. We went to speak to the tailors but they were reluctant to change both sets of mess dress without further payment. They were arguing that the cloth they used stated 'midnight blue' on the roll and that they believed they had made mess dress for other 29 Cdo guys from the same roll and no one had mentioned anything before – although they didn't seem to have the names of these guys handy for us to check this.

Eddie went to see the RSM and explained our predicament with the tailors and asked him to use his influence to get them to replace the mess dress without charge, because of his power to prevent other 29 Cdo guys from using their business in future. Of course, this provided one last opportunity before moving on to give me a little bit more constructive criticism for me to digest. He stated that due to the fact that I would never get past the rank of SSgt in the Army that it was unnecessary for me to have my mess dress replaced and that I should just make do with a slightly off-colour version for the rest of my Army career. Eddie duly went back and had his replaced and I made do with what I had. The cloth did darken a little over time and as most mess functions happened at night and indoors it was rarely noticed. On my dine out (leaving dinner) from 29 Cdo Regt, as is customary, I gave a little speech wearing this same mess dress. I told the story of why I was wearing it and what the previous RSM had said. I was now the senior Sergeant Major in 29 Cdo and I was leaving to become an RSM myself and I fully intended to, and did, wear my wrong-coloured mess dress in that job as well.

Some years later with the advent of Facebook I got a friend request from my old RSM. I have no idea if he wanted to kiss and make up or if he was just curious and wanted to have a look into my life, but I didn't accept. I doubt he has any idea just how much his negativity affected me. He would not have known that I was struggling emotionally when he decided he was going to make me pay for interfering with his 'train set'. I doubt he knew just how cutting and cruel his remarks were, but I do know that he was unkind and treated me unfairly. I told my half-sister Marion of his friend request and about his treatment of me over the years and she said that I should have accepted it and forgiven him. Marion is a regular church goer and clearly finds the forgiveness concept a lot easier than me. I don't doubt that it is better for the soul to forgive and forget, but he is not someone I think about very often now and I like it better this way – so I do not want him as a friend on Facebook. A couple of years later, I was on a night out in Glasgow with my dad and his friend Tommo when we bumped into him whilst he was out with another captain (he was a captain himself by then), and they were in Glasgow as that is where the Army Personnel centre is and they had business to do there.

I went through the motions of speaking to him although just being near him dragged up a lot of really negative emotions in me. My dad and Tommo were simply introduced to my previous BSM and RSM of 29 Cdo and because of their backgrounds they were happy to chat with him for a while. Afterwards, when I was able to, I told them a few of the things that had gone on with him and they wanted to go back and punch him. I stopped them from going back and confronting him as I was still serving and could have got into a lot of trouble over it, (as well as them), so let's just say he got off lightly!

A Long Way to Go

I was really chuffed about my promotion to Sergeant, but the disappointing thing at the time was that I was to be posted as a Sergeant to Arbroath in Scotland. This is where 7 Bty are based with 45 Commando Royal Marines. In Plymouth I was only 2.5 to 3 hours away from Swansea, which is where I would spend most of my weekends with Siân. I would now have to travel at weekends from Arbroath, which was a ten-hour plus journey. It was a little ironic that one of the big advantages of going to 29 Cdo initially was that I would be living close to Siân and a few years later I would end up so far away in Arbroath. I just had to suck it up and get on with it and commute at weekends. I wasn't the only one commuting, although most guys would be travelling to Plymouth, as that was where their wives and families were living. We would usually share a car and the driving and petrol costs, which made it a little easier, and I would get dropped off and picked up at Bristol Parkway en route and get a couple of trains to and from Swansea. As you can imagine, I would normally get in late on a Friday night and I would need to leave on Sunday afternoon to get a train to Bristol Parkway to meet the guys on the way back. It is a pretty monotonous journey and almost as soon as you get home on a Friday, you immediately start to dread the journey back on the Sunday, making it hard to relax. At the end of the day however, if you want to see your family you will do it – so that's what I did for that period of my life.

Apart from the travelling, 7 Bty was a good place as far as work was concerned, due to the fact that I was away from the Regimental Headquarters and therefore it was a much more relaxed environment to work in. One of the guys who was promoted to Sergeant at the same time as me was Mick from Liverpool, and 7 Bty was definitely his patch! What tended to happen in the Regiment was that Scots and Northern English guys often volunteered to serve in 7 Bty to be nearer their families and so many of the guys had spent the majority of their time in 29 Cdo there. Mick was definitely the Alpha male of the Battery and although we were the same rank, he threatened me in the first week because I hadn't attended the PT session that he wanted me to go on – he basically said that if I crossed him again, I would be sorry. Although Mick could be a little over-aggressive and confrontational at times, everyone respected him because he was very tough and a good soldier, and after this initial show of strength we got on fine.

Apart from the travelling, I had some reservations about 7 Battery because the SSGT, now WO2, who had not owned up on the Commando course was the BSM there. I had lost a lot of respect for him after the way I had seen him behave, but knew I would just have to get on with it with him as my boss. Although in my opinion his leadership style was autocratic, I did have sympathy for him as well because he was definitely not accepted by many people in 7 Bty. The fact that he had arrived in the Regiment and been promoted to WO2 automatically because he had already attended Gunnery Careers did not sit well with many. I have to admit that he may have adopted this leadership style as a coping mechanism due to the resistance and resentment towards him.

On Tour in the Balkans

Apart from an exercise in Bosnia for a month, which was interesting because I hadn't been to the Balkans before, the main event on the horizon was a six-month tour to Kosovo. We deployed to the capital of Kosovo, Pristina, in the autumn of 2000. The main aim of the tour was to promote stability in the region in the wake of the civil war in Kosovo which saw the Kosovo-Albanian people (who make up 95% of the population), gain independence from Serbia. The Serbs are predominantly a Christian people and the Kosovans are Muslim. Militarily the Serbs were much stronger than the Kosovans, so our main purpose was to prevent the Serbs – who did not want to relinquish control over Kosovo – from imposing themselves in the region as they had done previously. The war in the Balkans had been going on since the break-up of Yugoslavia in the 90s, and was mainly a war between the indigenous Christian Serbs in the region and the indigenous Muslims. It is well-documented and accepted that the Serbs were ruthless in their methods to maintain control of the Balkans, resorting to ethnic cleansing and mass murder. Eventually, the West intervened to protect the Muslims in order to allow free and democratic elections to take place in the region.

In Kosovo

As a former British soldier, it does anger me that so many people are quick to accuse the west of being anti-Muslim, and to be constantly waging war against Islam, as this was a war between Christians and Muslims and the West intervened to help the

Muslims, and actually took military action against the Serbs to bring an end to their ruthless domination of Muslims.

At the time, we occupied an old police station which would be our base for the duration of the tour. We would be operating as one of the companies of 45 Commando RM, and to make us up to full strength we were 'back-filled' by Royal Marines from 45 Cdo. This caused a little friction because of the 'them and us' type mentality, but by and large we got on pretty well. The guy who was the hardest to get along with was a Royal Marine Corporal called Cpl Darling. He was the most senior of the Royal Marines who joined us and he became their unofficial figurehead and the one the RM guys would go to. Cpl Darling had a bit of a tough guy attitude and he made it clear that he didn't like being with us and not with his own unit. I am sure it had been done countless times before, but I never tired of using every opportunity to thank him for absolutely anything by saying, "Thank you Darling." It definitely wound him up no end, but it was so much fun I couldn't resist it. It certainly made the tour pass a little quicker!

I attended a search advisors' course before the tour which meant I could go off with my team and conduct search operations which broke up the usual routine of patrolling the streets. The searches were mainly aimed at finding weapons in people's houses and taking them out of circulation. On one such search, my team and several others were working our way through a village where we had received a tip saying where a weapons cache might be. It was getting towards the end of the day and we hadn't found anything of any significance which was disappointing. We began to search a house that belonged to quite a scary-looking guy who was tall and well-built with a bald head. I recognised him as a guy I had stopped weeks earlier at a vehicle checkpoint (VCP) in a car with three other men, all carrying weapons that they didn't have a permit for, and he had a real attitude with me. After a stand-off, he handed me a mobile phone, and a well-spoken guy with an English accent who claimed to be a senior British officer, told me to let them go with their weapons. I was polite but said that I could not know if he was indeed an authentic British officer, so unless I was told from my own chain of command to allow the men to proceed with their weapons they were not going anywhere. The British guy was not happy with me at all: he said he would take it up with my chain of command and I would soon be told to let them go. I was ok with that so, in the meantime, my guys had their automatic weapons trained on the car and its occupants. After a few minutes, I got the call over the radio to let this guy and his men go with their weapons. I can only assume that the officer on the phone was genuine and he and these men were working with us in an unofficial way. I can remember the mocking look that he gave me as he drove away.

Now here he was again, although he did not seem to recognise me. His attitude was a little different this time and he was being very nice and polite, insisting that there was nothing illegal in his house. This just got me suspicious, so I decided we were going to do a really thorough search of the house and outbuildings. We searched for about half an hour without finding anything, and I was getting close to moving on to the next house when one of the lads brought something to my attention. In many of the gardens there were piles of bricks and these bricks had makeshift roofs over them, presumably to keep the bricks dry although I didn't really understand why this was necessary. The roof that was on this man's stack of bricks was nicer than anyone else's and looked very well made. I decided that this warranted a closer look and so we got a ladder up and started to dismantle the roof to look inside. The man now went from polite and calm to extremely agitated, which is how

I remembered him from the last time. I couldn't be sure if he was getting upset because we were causing him future work in putting his roof back. The reason soon became clear as we discovered a very significant weapons cache. Sealed in thick clear polythene bags were dozens of AK 47 automatic rifles, rocket-propelled grenades, hand grenades and a lot of ammunition. As well as the weapons there was a considerable amount of cash in German Deutsche Marks. I placed the man under arrest and called for RMP (Royal Military Police) assistance and this time I was not handed a phone with a British Officer on the line telling me to let him go. Clearly on this occasion having this stash was not part of whatever the arrangement was with our side. Maybe he would be released by friends in high places further down the line, but that was for others to decide. Whilst we were waiting for the RMP to arrive, we asked him how much money was there but he said he didn't know because it wasn't his money, or his weapons. We counted it and there was 67,000 Marks which was still legal tender before the advent of the Euro. As he was taken away by the RMP I resisted the temptation to give him a similar look to the one he had given me as he drove away from the VCP – honest!

As well as conducting search operations in order to disarm the local population we also patrolled as a unit in vehicles 24/7. At the time there were a number of kidnappings at gunpoint for ransom taking place and we were hoping to be able to intervene and put a stop to this activity if we could. One evening, in the early hours, a vehicle screeched past us on a dirt track heading in the opposite direction and so I told my driver to get after it asap. My driver, a Marine called Rob, attempted to turn the vehicle in one go, but unfortunately the turning circle of the Snatch Land Rover we were in is pretty big and so Rob had to knock it into reverse for a few feet before he could carry on in pursuit. Unfortunately, whilst doing this an iron picket that was protruding from the dirt at the side of the road pierced the skin of the Land Rover which delayed us for a few more seconds and we were then unable to catch up with the suspicious speeding vehicle again. I put that one down to experience and reported the incident in my patrol report on my return to base.

As you can imagine these Land Rovers are being worked pretty hard and damage is inevitable which was causing problems because damage wasn't being reported so that repairs could take place. It would have been easy for me to not report the damage because the hole was very hard to spot. After a couple of days the vehicle would have been used by many drivers and so it would be impossible to pinpoint who had caused the damage. I had no intention of doing this however, so I reported the damage to the Royal Marine motor transport sergeant who would organise the repair to be done. He thanked me for bringing it to his attention as most people weren't bothering to and I thought no more of it. About a week later however, I was told that Rob as the driver and me as the Commander of the vehicle would be going in front of the CO to be charged for the damage to the vehicle. At first, I thought this was a wind-up but my BSM told me it was true. I argued that this damage occurred whilst attempting to apprehend at the very least a very dangerous driver, which was our job, but my complaint fell on deaf ears. I felt completely betrayed. I had done the right thing and reported the damage which was surely caused with mitigating circumstances. I felt let down by my BSM and my Battery Commander because I believe they should have stuck up for me and Rob, and if necessary, got our own chain of command involved to fight our corner. By this, I mean get the CO of 29 Cdo to speak to the CO of 45 Cdo who we were 'on loan' to and get him to see sense. I firmly believed that if I had been a Royal Marine Sergeant, this would not be happening and that we were being thrown to the wolves. We both went on CO's Orders and were both fined £200 each. Unbelievable! The charge was that I failed to get out of the vehicle in order to properly oversee the reversing manoeuvre as per standing orders and that Rob failed to insist that I get out and do this. Technically, I could not argue against this but if the CO wanted to catch soldiers committing this offence, then he just needed to look out of his window at the car park for five minutes: he would see lots of guilty drivers and commanders doing it. I would also be utterly amazed if he always adhered to this rule himself with his driver. Obviously, out of respect, I was unable to say this to the CO but in my statement, I did ask him to use his discretionary powers to overturn the charge under the circumstances; also, because making an example of us would deter others from ever reporting any damage to the vehicles which would ultimately undermine our operational effectiveness as a unit. My plea fell on deaf ears, which left a very bitter taste in my mouth.

Under normal circumstances I would definitely have appealed against this decision because it was so blatantly unfair, but I was faced with a bit of a dilemma at the time. I had put in my application to go on SAS selection which began towards the end of the tour and the 45 Cdo RSM said to me that if I contested the decision, he would delay me from leaving to go on selection, which would mean I would have to wait at least another six months. I was very unhappy with being treated this way again by my superiors, and I really wanted to appeal immediately which would have annoyed the CO and RSM, but I wanted to go on selection more, so I decided to let it go.

SAS

I got back to the UK just before Christmas which was a massive bonus to be able to spend time with Siân and my family before attending the course in January 2001. I do not want to go into much detail about the course itself due to the Official Secrets Act but there are others, rightly or wrongly, who have written about the course and what it entails. So I am sure you will be able to find out more information about it elsewhere without too much difficulty. I reported to Sennybridge training camp in South Wales which is the base for the initial phase of the course. Physically I was in good shape and I was able to cope with that side of things quite well. Yes, it was very tough at times but that was to be expected. Most of the course in the first four weeks is conducted on the Brecon Beacons and the Elan Valley. There are two courses a year which are either in the winter or summer. I deliberately chose a winter course because even though it's in the Welsh mountains, it can still get pretty hot in the summer, and I did not want to have to complete the long hard marches over the mountains during hot weather. In recent years, there have been instances of guys actually dying whilst on the course due to overheating whilst pushing themselves beyond the limit because of hot weather.

A downside to doing a winter course is that the visibility is much poorer, so your map reading skills need to be very good in order to navigate yourself from checkpoint to checkpoint over hills against the clock. Although fitness-wise I was feeling ok, my knees were not holding up that well and were becoming really sore. One of the guys suggested that I use Glucosamine Sulphate as this helps with joint pain and this did help quite a bit and probably kept me on the course for a few more weeks.

By week 4, I was limping quite badly and was unable to complete some of the tests inside the required time, so I was Returned to Unit (RTU'd) and had to leave the course. Although disappointed, I knew from experience that I could come back from this, so I decided to try again the following year.

Coming Home

On hearing that I would be returning to 29 Cdo, the Regiment decided to send me to 8 Bty in Plymouth instead of returning me to 7 Bty. Apart from the travelling at weekends I had enjoyed my time in Arbroath because it was a totally different and more relaxed environment being away from the hierarchy of the Regiment in Plymouth. It felt much nicer being back in the Citadel as a sergeant because I was now moving in more grown-up circles and I felt less of a 'fish out of water' as I had felt as a JNCO there. The next big thing on the horizon for 8 Bty was a long, mainly seaborne deployment around the Mediterranean for several months, and I was due to finish just prior to Xmas leave. The main problem for me was this was going to cause issues with preparing properly to go back on SAS selection again in January 2002. I wasn't sure how I was going to overcome this situation, but the BSM announced something on parade that was going to give me a better chance of preparing properly. 8 Bty were due to provide a sergeant to go to Larkhill to work with the School of Artillery for a two-year posting starting after Easter leave. I approached the BSM and told him that I would like to volunteer for it because I would have plenty of time to train for selection. His advice was that it was probably not the best move for me career-wise, and although I knew he was right I still wanted to do it to give myself the best chance of passing, so he agreed. And so, six years after leaving Larkhill I was back again in 34 Bty, but this time wearing a green beret which felt good. I didn't put my application in immediately for the next winter SAS selection as I didn't want it to be too obvious of my intentions and reasons for going there.

The other advantage to not going away with 8 Bty was the fact that I could spend a lot more time with Siân in Swansea. It was only a couple of hours' drive in the car and so I spent most weekends and leave periods there. The advantage to Siân now living in South Wales was that I could easily travel from Swansea and do some good training in the Brecon Beacons, and get back the same day.

It was during this time that I met a girl whose mum lived in the house next to my mum's. She was a school teacher and we became friends which soon went on to become a relationship. She was 5 years older than me but I did not regard that as an issue and I was feeling happy for the first time in a long while. She was very keen to move the relationship along and it wasn't long before we were talking about me moving in with her and her daughter at their house. So, after only a few weeks of going out, I moved in with her. Not long after that, she started to talk about Siân coming to live with us as well. Although it seemed very soon, Siân was very fond of her and she was very happy when she learnt that we were a couple. I remember the time when Siân first saw us holding hands which made her beam, because she knew that this meant we were a couple. I liked the idea of Siân living with me as part of a conventional family set-up and so, even though it was all a bit quick, I agreed. My mum approved of my girlfriend at the time and so when I spoke to her about it, she liked the idea. So we made plans for Siân to move in with us in the following year (2002).

Go Again

After a couple of months at Larkhill, I decided that the time was right to put my application in for the next winter SAS course. I had been expecting a negative response to this but it seemed to pass without incident, or so I thought. After a couple of months, it was autumn and I had not yet received a joining instruction from the SAS, which was odd. I called the SAS Training Wing and they said the reason I hadn't received a joining instruction was that they hadn't received my application! They said that if I wanted to get on the next course, then I had less than 2 weeks to get my application in. Obviously, my application could have got lost in the post, but instead of simply submitting another I wanted to know that my application wasn't being blocked by 34 Bty in some way. This would have been against the rules in the Army in that it is forbidden to block an application to the SAS no matter what the circumstances, and so all units must submit an application. I asked to speak to the Battery Commander to gauge his opinion on the matter. He, in a matter-of-fact way, told me that the reason the SAS hadn't received the application is that he had stopped it being sent. This was a very awkward situation for me to be in because the BC was very senior to me, and my immediate urge was to demand an explanation, but that would not have been appropriate. I did ask why and his reason was that the CO had a policy that all non-infantry applicants for the course should complete an infantry skills course prior to attending SAS selection.

I explained to the BC that the SAS training wing had already given me an exemption from doing that prior to re-attending selection because my Commando training was a lot more advanced than the infantry skills course itself. Instead of conceding this point, he simply repeated, "It is the CO's policy that all non-infantry applicants complete an infantry skills course prior to attending the course." I knew at this point that I was being blocked, but I did not know if it was by the BC alone or by the CO as well. That evening, I was having a pint with a friend and the Regimental Training Officer, who was a Sergeant Major, asked me if I was ok as I was looking a bit fed up. I explained to him about my dilemma with the course application. I knew that I could report to the SAS the fact that my unit was refusing to submit my application, but I knew that this would cause trouble.

You have to expect that you will not pass – because the fact is that most don't – and be returned to unit, so the last thing you want to do is to completely alienate your unit in case you do return. He said he would speak to the Adjutant, who was a captain, who worked very closely with and for the CO, to find out if the CO was also involved in this. The RTO got back to me the next day and said that the CO knew nothing about my application and was angry that the BC had not submitted it as per the rules, and he had ordered the BC to submit it immediately. Later that day, the BC summoned me to his office and announced that he had some good news! He said that he had managed to convince the CO to let me go on Selection and to waive his requirement for me to do the infantry skills course. Integrity is a big part of being a leader of men, but unfortunately this man was showing none. I found it very difficult to be respectful to him: I think I managed to just say, "Oh that's good, Sir," or words to that effect, and I left his office feeling relieved and disgusted at the same time.

Unsurprisingly I did not get a very good Confidential Report (CR) from him that year which is what is used to decide whether to promote someone or not. It was too early for me to be promoted anyway, but if I failed selection and returned to the Artillery this CR would not help me at all. Incredibly, he wrote that: "Sgt Poneskis is too easily distracted away from his primary role, which is a Gun number one in 34 Bty." If I had been easily distracted by alcohol or drugs or petty crime, then I could have understood his disapproval, but the fact is that everyone that has ever joined the SAS has definitely been distracted from their previous (primary) employment, otherwise there wouldn't be anyone in the SAS! Unbelievable.

A few weeks later, the Twin Towers were struck and the military action that followed in Iraq and Afghanistan would dramatically affect the careers of most British servicemen and women for many years to come. For the time being my Army life continued as normal and I soon received my 'joining instructions' for the January 2002 selection course. My preparation for the course had gone very well and I arrived for the course at Sennybridge camp in better shape physically than I had the previous year. During the first three weeks, my knees started to cause me problems once more. A doctor I know used a needle to inject cortisone directly into my knees in an attempt to reduce the inflammation that was causing me to limp badly again, but it was not enough. I passed the first two tests on week four relatively easily, but on the third day my knees blew up on me and I began to limp badly again. It was now February in the Brecon Beacons and the weather was cold and wet. Under normal circumstances, when moving across this terrain at pace carrying a heavy Bergan in the winter, staying warm was not a problem. In fact, you had to be very careful not to overheat. Unfortunately for me, I was now limping and not able to move very fast, so I began to get cold. When I arrived at my next checkpoint, the instructor knew that I was well behind time and limping badly, so he decided that it was not safe to allow me to carry on and told me to get in the back of his Land Rover and not continue. So my second attempt to get into the SAS would also end in disappointment. Unless there are exceptional circumstances, the SAS will only allow two attempts at selection, so I would not be allowed to try again. But in any case, I now knew that my knees were probably not up to the challenge. If my knees had been up to it, who knows if I would have been able to pass all of the other various tests that took place after the Hill Phase. I would now never know. I was very disappointed at the time but there is a phrase that I've heard that I like a lot because it applies to many things in life and that is: *it's better to try and fail, than to fail to try.*

Proving My Worth

Now that a career in the SAS was closed to me, I did some soul-searching about what I really wanted to do next. It's only when one door is firmly shut to you that you are able to properly decide what you want to do next. I now realised that I really wanted to become a late-entry Officer in 29 Commando and to prove to myself and all those who doubted me that I was capable and worthy of achieving such an ambition! With my new-found drive and determination, I returned to 34 Bty and decided to knuckle down and do my best to get promoted to the next rank up which is Staff Sergeant. Now, all I had to do was win over the BC to get him to write me a good CR which would be my 3rd as a Sergeant (Sgt), and once you have three CRs as a Sgt you were eligible for promotion. I had about six months of work to do before CRs were due again and although I knew it wouldn't be easy with the Major, I decided to give it my best shot.

Family Stability?

Later that year, Siân also moved in with me and she enrolled at the local primary school aged 9. I now felt that Siân's and my life had a real sense of normality in that we were now part of a normal family set-up with Siân living in what felt like a more typical household. I soon became very fond of my girlfriend's daughter and I would love making her and Siân laugh. I had a little rhyme which was "Fee fi fo fum: I'm going to catch you and tickle your tums." I would then make a dastardly menacing laughing sound whilst they both ran off screeching and laughing to try and escape me. Once caught and lightly tickled, they would say, "Again, again," wanting to play the game for hours it seemed!

I am sorry to say that the harmony in the relationship started to become a little strained and we began to argue about little things quite a lot. I thought it might be that my girlfriend was feeling insecure about how committed I was to our new family, so I sought to reassure her and made plans to propose and I bought a ring in preparation. I remember going out for a few drinks with one of her relatives and confiding in them about my plans to propose, and he let slip that she had been married twice before which was a little embarrassing for both of us because I didn't know about her first husband. I spoke to her about it and she said that it was a very short-lived marriage and it had been a mistake; that's why she hadn't mentioned it. She apologised for not telling me about it and said that she hadn't told me because she was embarrassed, which I understood, so we didn't mention it again.

Towards the end of the year, we went on a family holiday and it was then that I proposed. She said yes, and so the date was set for the summer of 2003. Back in 34 Bty, I was working really hard and I know for a fact that I was performing very well. But it seems I had well and truly burned my bridges with the Battery Commander and he wrote me a really bad (CR) again. He rated me at the 'lower end of the middle third' of sergeants in 34 Bty which gave me no chance of promotion, as only those at the 'higher end of the top third' are likely to be promoted. This was pretty bad news for me careerwise because as things stood, with the length of service I had left in the Army, I could not now reach the rank of WO1/Regimental Sergeant

Major and beyond. Now that a career in the SAS had gone, it seemed that my ambition of becoming an Officer in 29 Commando had gone too. I felt a little lost at this time in the Army and didn't know what to do for the best, and I did consider leaving, but I could not think of anything else that I wanted to do that would provide a regular income. So I decided to stick it out a little longer.

War Stories

The Harsh Reality of War

Things began to look up a bit at work when a new BC took over who in my opinion was a very good officer. I started to get recognition from him for my efforts and he reassured me that I was doing well and to keep it up. It was now early 2003 and I had about six months of my two years left in 34 Bty. I decided that all I could do from now on in the Army was my very best, and I would see where that took me.

The second Iraq war was about to take place which was being justified by the Bush administration as retribution for the 9/11 attacks. 29 Cdo were preparing to go to war at the time, but as things stood, I was in 34 Bty and not available to go. The Regiment made a formal request to have me and all other 29 Cdo guys released from 34 Bty to try and deploy with as many good men as possible. All of the guys in my gun detachment were from 29 Cdo and we all wanted to go to war. It's an odd thing to try to explain, especially when you have a family, but in times of war most soldiers want to go, even though they might tell their wives and girlfriends otherwise. I don't know how female soldiers feel about this as I haven't spoken to any about it. At this time, there was a virtual tug of war going on between 14 Regt/34 Bty and 29 Cdo Regt over us.

At one point, it was decided that only I would go from my detachment, and my guys were pretty mad about this I can tell you! I have no idea what deals were done, but I was later informed that I would in fact be staying with 34 Bty and all of my guys would go to war instead. I obviously had mixed emotions about this due to Siân mainly, but I was feeling pretty gutted about it at the time. I can remember very clearly the day that a vehicle containing four non-commando 34 Bty guys arrived on the gun position where we were firing on Larkhill ranges. The men got out and took over from my guys on the Gun. It was really difficult saying goodbye and good luck to them, then seeing them disappear down the range road and off to war without me.

The main ground invasion of Iraq began in the early hours of 21st March 2003, but all I could do was watch the war unfold on the TV like everyone else. The news broke later on that day that a US helicopter had crashed carrying eight British personnel, but I reassured myself that there were 28,000 British troops deployed over there, so the chances of it being anyone I knew were small. Tragically, my optimism was misplaced because I later found out that three 29 Cdo guys from 148 Bty had died in the crash. They were Les Hehir aged 34, Llewelyn Evan (Welly) aged 24 and Ian Seymour aged 28. I had only met Ian a few times, but I knew that he was married with a five-year-old boy. I had become friends with Les when we were both in 8 Bty for a while. He was genuinely the nicest guy you could hope to meet, and he was also married with two young sons. The death of Welly hit me hard because he had been one of the guys on my Gun detachment during Ocean Wave. Welly was so positive and full of life, it was infectious; you just could not help feeling a little happier if he was around. How could Welly, who was engaged to be married, possibly be dead at 24 years old? I was asked a few days later if I wanted to carry Welly's coffin at his funeral which would be held in his home town of Llandudno in North Wales and I accepted.

The funeral was one of the hardest things I have ever experienced. It was such a sad day attending the funeral for such a well-loved person. I had never carried a coffin for a full military honour's funeral before, and I did not foresee how hard I would find it emotionally. All around, people were allowing their grief to pour out, but whilst carrying the coffin in and out of the church in full dress uniform at a military honours funeral you have a job to do. You have to keep in step with the other five pallbearers and perform certain Drill movements in time with the others and so you have to keep it together. During the ceremony, the five of us sat in front of the congregation close to the coffin which was immaculately covered by the Union Flag, with Welly's Commando beret and medals placed on top. The readings were particularly hard to listen to whilst trying not to cry. Welly's best friend, who was also a local lad, described him perfectly in that although he could be mischievous and try to wind people up a lot, it was impossible to stay mad at him for long. His friend said that after he had joined the Army he would come home and insist on singing *American Pie* (the song that I spent hours trying to teach him in South Africa) at the slightest opportunity even though his singing was rubbish and he could never get the words right. His friend then said, "If only I could hear Welly sing *American Pie* once more." Tears ran down my face at this point, but apart from that, I managed to keep myself in check.

After the service, we carried the coffin back to the hearse and travelled to the cemetery where our final duty was to lower the coffin into the ground whilst his nearest and dearest were weeping uncontrollably. A bugler then sounded *the Last Post* which was followed by a gun salute by the honour guard.

Afterwards, there was a wake in the town which we attended still wearing our uniforms, but I had to sneak off and find a quiet alleyway where I completely broke down and sobbed uncontrollably. I didn't need to keep my emotions in check any more.

Welly as a young happy soldier

Picture: Welly on operations

Me carrying Welly's coffin – middle pall bearer on the right side of the picture

Another hard day was to follow because the funeral for Les would take place the next day in Poole in Dorset. Ian's funeral had been a couple of days before that, but I was unable to attend due to pallbearer rehearsals taking place in Plymouth at the same time. I had no function to perform this time other than to attend the funeral which was a relief. The enduring image that I will never forget from that day was the sight of Les' two young sons, aged five and three, following his coffin – covered with the Union Flag with his Beret and Medals on top – out of the church with their mum. I will never forget that till the day I die.

After the initial phase and the overthrow of Saddam Hussein, the British Military remained in Iraq for a further six years to try to maintain law and order, but 29 Cdo did not ever deploy there again so nor did I, although members of my family did. My brother John had served in the first Gulf War in Iraq in 1990 and my sister Debbie also deployed there.

In the meantime, in 34 Bty I did my job to the best of my ability and I got my CR from the new BC and he ranked me his best sergeant out of 20 (34 Bty was at the time much larger than a normal Bty and therefore had a larger number of sergeants). I felt relief more than anything that a different superior had endorsed me, although I couldn't help feeling that it was too little too late. I had taken a gamble going back to 34 Bty to give myself the best chance of getting into the SAS, but it hadn't paid off, and I hadn't been able to get back on track career-wise. At least I could return to 29 Cdo/8 Bty with my head held high on the back of a good CR though, and not a rubbish one!

In the years to come, the Iraq war would go on to claim 179 British lives in total and, unbelievably, 4,497 Americans. I cannot speak for the Americans, but as a British citizen we were told that the reason for this war was Iraq having weapons of mass destruction (WMDs) and these were in the hands of Saddam Hussein who had already used chemical weapons on his own civilian population. As a soldier I supported the war because of the threat this posed for the world, and soldiers are willing to put their lives on the line under such circumstances. When it later became clear that the Weapons of Mass Destruction claim was simply not true, I know I was not alone in feeling very angry about this war. I am not a big conspiracy theorist but I share the view of many that the British and American people were lied to about WMDs in Iraq. Les, Welly, Ian and thousands of other troops, as well as thousands of Iraqis should not have lost their lives fighting for this lie, and as far as I am concerned, that leaves those in power at the time in Britain and America, with the blood of these people on their hands.

Getting Hitched

My commute at weekends now took about two and a half hours on a good run. Siân seemed much more settled – I think mainly because she had more of a routine and the school she was now attending was much better than her previous one, which as any parent knows makes a big difference. I got married in the Royal Citadel in July 2003. On the surface to others, I am sure everything seemed ok, but behind the scenes we argued badly before and on our wedding day: we went on our honeymoon barely speaking and continued to argue whilst away. I think we both knew that we had made a big mistake, but when we returned, we tried to make it work and acted happy for the sake of the kids, and as far as the rest of the world was concerned, we were ok. With hindsight, I know that we were not compatible enough to get married but I suppose, like many, I buried my head in the sand and ignored the issues between us. I had ploughed on naïvely hoping that the regular arguments would subside once we were married. I wrongly pinned my hopes on her unhappiness being down to me not showing enough commitment to her and the family, but in the end getting married did not help things at all.

Raising Money for Charity

Later that year (November 2003), I agreed to do the New York Marathon with my dad and help him raise money for his chosen charity, MENCAP, and between us we managed to raise about £5,000. I was quite lucky in that the landlords of the two main pubs that 29 Cdo guys go to on the Barbican in Plymouth helped me raise a lot of my money. Pete from The Three Crowns put on a fundraising evening for me and provided food which raised over £500 and John from The Navy Inn actually wrote me a personal cheque for £500!

Whilst in New York, we kept bumping into two sisters from Scotland who were also running the marathon. Apparently, they noticed my dad's accent which sounded very similar to their own, and it transpired that they were from the same town in Scotland. We got on well together during our time in New York. I have to admit that I was attracted to one of them, and I knew that she was attracted to me, but I was married and she was also in a relationship. So we did nothing but talk during our time in New York, but we did stay in touch for a while which wasn't really appropriate.

My dad and I stayed on in Manhattan for a few more days to do some tourist stuff. We took in a Broadway show which was pretty cool. The show was Cabaret which was quite raunchy at times and I remember feeling a little embarrassed being sat next to my dad during some of raunchy scenes. I needn't have worried because when I looked to see how he was coping with the sexual content, he was fast asleep.

We went on a boat trip around the Statue of Liberty which is a spectacular sight. We also visited Ground Zero which is where the Twin Towers of the World Trade Centre once stood which was both shocking and disturbing to see. Whilst looking down into those two huge holes in the ground, it was hard to contemplate that as well as all of the lives lost on 9/11, the same event was the catalyst for the Iraq war which had already claimed the lives of Les, Welly, and Ian. Little did I know standing there that hundreds of other British service personnel would go on to lose their lives in Iraq and Afghanistan, and some of these people who were yet to die I would know personally and care for a lot.

Promotion

Back at work I settled in nicely in 8 Bty, which was made a lot easier due to having a really good BSM. After a winter deployment to Norway in 2004, I was promoted to Staff Sergeant in the spring. But this time I was posted to 79 Bty which meant that I would now serve as a SNCO (Sgt) in all 3 Gun Btys of 29 Cdo Regt in quite a short space of time.

I had a few months in the UK before going away to America for a two-and-a-half-month deployment in May. Things had settled down at home: I was getting on ok at work and Siân was happy, so things were good at last! I felt totally at home in 79 Bty in that I really liked the BC Richard Smith and the BSM Dave Thatcher, which helped! I was now given the job in camp of Battery Training Warrant Officer which is the job of a Sergeant Major (next rank up) and involved organising and arranging all of the training courses that members of the Bty would go on. On exercise (out of camp practising for war), I was doing the job of Assistant Reconnaissance Officer (ARO) which I really enjoyed too. In doing ARO, I worked closely with a young captain called Jim who was the Battery Reconnaissance Officer (BRO) and we got on really well both professionally and socially. Jim would often get in trouble with the hierarchy of the Regiment because let's just say in those days he was a bit of a maverick. But once he calmed down a bit and worked with the system and not against it, he became an outstanding officer and real leader of men.

For the first time in my Army career, I felt comfortable in my surroundings because I now enjoyed my job and who I was working with, instead of it just being a job.

Family Breakdown

In May of that year, I said my goodbyes my family and went off to America with 79 Bty to go on exercise with the US Marine Corps. I phoned home regularly to check in, but my wife began to get more and more distant with me. I tried to block it out and reassured myself that she was probably just fed up that I was away and that it would be ok when I got back. But I was wrong.

Siân seemed to be spending more and more time away at her friend's house, which was another warning sign. I got back to the UK in late July and whilst I was in the car on my way home, my mum called me and said that she believed that my wife was having an affair. I must admit that I felt sick in my stomach because I knew in my heart it was true because of the way she had been on the phone with me. The guy in question was someone I had met with my wife at a nearby medieval village and he would play the part of a Welsh knight in mock battles.

When I got home, both girls greeted me but there was definitely something wrong. Siân was really pleased to see me but my wife and her daughter were very uncomfortable around me and it was clear that there was a big problem. I knew what my mum had said but she didn't know for sure and I wondered if it had just been a good friendship that had gone too far. I wanted to find out for sure before jumping to any conclusions.

Later on, when the girls were not around, I asked my wife if she had been seeing anyone whilst I had been away and she said no. When it was appropriate to do so, I asked Siân what had been going and what she told me was very disturbing. My wife's 'friend' had started staying over at the house not long after I had gone and, incredibly, they would take Siân and my wife's daughter for days out and for meals together. Siân even said that they would hold hands whilst with the girls. I instantly remembered that Siân knew about us being a couple when she saw us holding hands. This made me feel sick and angry at the same time, but more than that I felt so sad about what it must have felt like for Siân at 11 years old whilst her father was far away. This is why Siân was spending so much time at her friend's house and I am so grateful to this family because they knew what was happening and they wanted to shelter Siân as much as they could.

I firmly believe that there are certain rules you simply do not break when it comes to children and this was definitely one of them. If adults decide that they do not want to be with each other any more, yes it can be tough, but that's life and I can accept that. But you can and must keep children out of it as much as possible, because to do otherwise is utterly selfish and extremely cruel on the kids.

I logged on to the family computer and although I did not know her log-in details it was early days for computer privacy so I could see in the internet registry what emails were passing between them. It was clear they had been having a full-blown affair for quite some time. When I confronted her with this proof, she was unable to deny it any longer. I told her that I would pack our things and we would both be leaving asap. Siân was really upset to be leaving her step sister (as I was), because they had bonded, but she was not sorry to be leaving her stepmother. It seems even before I had gone away to America, she had cooled considerably towards Siân. But Siân had not told me and put a brave face on it for my sake.

So, unceremoniously and with neighbours looking on, I loaded the car with our personal stuff and we left for Plymouth to stay with my mum. I am not going to labour on about how this all felt, as it felt terrible and that's that.

I had one last thing I needed to go back and collect from the house: a soft top car that I had bought for my wife from a soldier returning from Germany – but it turned out he hadn't imported it legally and so it had to be returned. I drove from Plymouth to Swansea to stay with my dad and the next day he drove me to get the car. He was feeling pretty angry about how my wife had in particular treated Siân. We collected the car and my wife was there but neither of us spoke to her. I had a lot of anger in me, and I really wanted to shout at someone, but I did not want to intimidate or be aggressive towards a woman. Instead, I decided that I would go and see the man she had the affair with.

I tried to go and see him on my own but my dad insisted on coming along. I told Dad that I just wanted to tell him what I thought of him and hopefully thoroughly embarrass him in front of his work colleagues. I didn't know if I was going to hit him if I am honest; I decided I would start off with a really good verbal assault on him and see what happened next. When I got there, I spotted him in a Land Rover about to drive away. I got his attention and told him I wanted a word. I will give him his due, he didn't shy away from a confrontation with me, and he must have expected a fight was likely to happen. His friend, who also got out of the Land Rover, was a really big muscular guy – about 17- 18 stone, which is maybe why he was feeling so brave. He was a few inches shorter than me but probably the same weight and he looked as though he had been building himself up since I had been away. I immediately got into his face and I really lost my temper calling him every name under the sun. I said to him that making his affair so obvious to Siân was lower than low. Making it so obvious that he was staying the night, the four of them going out together for days out and holding hands in front of Siân was unforgivable. One thing I hadn't planned on was that in spelling it out so graphically just how cruel and heartless he had been towards Siân, my dad, who was 64 at the time lost his temper, pushed me out of the way and punched him in the face.

The big fella immediately went to step in and I am not sure what move my dad did, but he made the guy lose his balance and in the next instant he was on the floor. I decided that it had already gone far enough, and I said to my dad that we should go. It felt good to have let off some steam, but I was also a little worried they might report the incident to the police and I was right.

Later that day, I received a phone call from a police officer demanding that my dad and I report to the police station to answer an accusation of assault, adding that there were several witnesses. I spoke to my dad about it and he was quite happy to hand himself in, so to speak, but I didn't want to play ball. I am pretty sure that if the incident did go to court that the papers would get involved. The main ingredients of the story would have been: *school teacher has an affair with a make-believe Welsh knight whilst her husband is away with the Army and when the soldier returns there is a fight and the soldier's 64-year-old ex-SAS father punches the man and fells his 17/18 stone wing man*!

I didn't really want the publicity and it would not help me convince my superiors that my personal life was stable which was always strongly considered when deciding someone's suitability for promotion. I decided to call my wife's sister who was a really nice person and I told her that she should advise them to call off the police because of the inevitable publicity. She agreed that would be for the best and, unsurprisingly after that, the charges were dropped!

The immediate issue I had to face was: where would Siân live? I had a room in the Sergeants' Mess (accommodation and dining facility for SNCOs) but Siân could not live there. I did not want Siân to move back in with my mum as she was approaching teenage years and I didn't think that would be fair on either of them.

The obvious solution was boarding school and I knew that there were some really good private ones in and around Plymouth.

My sister Debbie came to the rescue at this point because she contacted the two best boarding schools in the area and arranged interviews for Siân with the respective headmasters. Debbie took time out of her busy schedule as a Lieutenant Colonel to travel down to Plymouth to attend the headmaster interviews with Siân and I. It was very short notice to try and get into a really good school and so we knew we would have to create a really good impression to convince them to allocate a place. The first school interview was at Plymouth College which is a private boarding school right in the centre of Plymouth, very close to my camp and my mum's, who had since moved back to Plymouth. I remember saying to Siân that at some point the headmaster might ask her if she had any questions for him, and I suggested she ask if she could study another foreign language as an extracurricular choice if possible. As I suspected, the headmaster did indeed ask Siân if she had any questions for him, to which she asked if she would be allowed to wear heels and make-up to school. He smiled and said, "Yes, very small-heeled shoes and a tiny bit of makeup." We were very impressed with the school and the headmaster and we were delighted when he offered Siân a place in Year 7 starting in September. We decided not to go ahead with the second school interview as it was about 30 minutes out of town and Plymouth College ticked all of our boxes. The really cool thing about Siân being a boarder at this school was that I could see her during lunchtimes, as well as after school and of course at weekends. I started to see Siân more now, which was great, and Siân could also spend more time with my mum too. Siân loved it at Plymouth

College and she thrived there. She missed her stepsister badly for years to come, which was heart-breaking, but there was nothing I could do about it. Siân had had quite a turbulent upbringing up to that point and she badly needed some stability in her life and also some really positive adult guidance which she got from this school in spades. I know that there were many excellent teachers who helped Siân over the next seven years, but two deserve a special thank you: Martin and Mary Tippets, who were Siân's House Masters which means that they also lived in the boarding house and after school (when they were normal teachers) they performed the role of parent to dozens of boarders aged 11 to 18. Martin and Mary took a lot of time to counsel Siân who at times, quite understandably, was a mixed-up child and she benefitted greatly from their dedication, kindness, wisdom and patience.

Although it was very soon after the split, I thought a lot about the lady I'd met in New York. I wished I could have met her when I was single but the timing just hadn't worked out like that. We hadn't been in touch for a long time and she may well have moved on, but I decided to call her and tell her what had happened. We chatted for a while and although she was still upset with me for breaking off contact previously, she accepted that I had been putting Siân first and so she decided to put it behind us.

When we first met up, I didn't know how it would go, but pretty soon we relaxed around each other and we became a couple. When we got more serious, she was really nervous about meeting Siân. But Siân took a shine to her immediately and they have maintained a really good relationship to this day. She eventually moved to Plymouth and we moved in to one of my flats. In theory, Siân could have now lived with us in our flat, but I wanted us to settle properly as a couple before exploring that scenario. If Siân had been unhappy as a boarder at Plymouth College, I would obviously have addressed the situation and had her home with me regardless of any strain it might have put on my early relationship. But the fact was that Siân was loving being a boarder, so there was no need to upset the apple cart at this point! The other thing to consider was that Plymouth College was a private school and the Army would only contribute towards the fees if Siân boarded; they would not fork out for her to get a private education as a day pupil.

Promotion Again?

Now that I had got my private affairs in order, I was able to concentrate on my Army career again. I know I had only just been promoted to SSgt but it was possible to be promoted to WO2 after only one year in rank and I decided to give it my best shot. Jim and I worked really well together which helped us impress our bosses whilst on exercise. I also put into practice – something that I believe is very important in any job environment and that is to view being given a task by your boss not as a chore, but an opportunity! In the Army the term for being given a task, or extra work to do, is known as being 'dicked' to do something. The reality is that if you accept this extra work without complaining and carry out the work to the best of your ability as soon as you can (hopefully before the deadline given), you will impress your boss no end. So, when it comes to promotion time, you will be head and shoulders above your competition – and I am sure this is the case in any job!

I can remember when Dave the BSM went away for a week, he had work that needed to be done whilst away. He informed me and two other SSgts that he had left a list of jobs to be carried out on his desk and he would appreciate it if between us we would get the jobs done whilst he was away. During the week I looked at the list and asked the other two if they wanted to take any of the jobs but they were not really interested, so I went ahead and got them all done myself. When the BSM returned, he came to see me and said he was really impressed with the work that had been done and asked me what I had done from the list. I told him that the others had been busy and so I had done the jobs, to which he nodded thoughtfully and walked away. I continued to do my very best and later on that year I received another really good report. The report ranked me as number one of all of the SSgts in the Regiment. This report would go to the promotion board to decide if I would promote again the following year.

The promotion board took place early the following year (2005) and I was absolutely delighted to get promoted to Sergeant Major and also remain in 79 Bty. Things had turned around quickly for me since being in the doldrums in 34 Bty as a Sergeant, and now I had managed to go from Sergeant to Sergeant Major in one year, back in 29 Cdo Regiment. As is often the case in the Army after a promotion, my job didn't change at all in 79 Bty in that I continued to do the job of Battery Training Warrant Officer in camp and Bty Guide on exercise. The first exercise I did as a Sergeant Major was an Artillery exercise which initially took place in Wales before moving on to Salisbury Plain.

Jim and I continued to work well together and I was really enjoying the job of reconnaissance because you have a lot of independence from the rest of the Bty. Tragically on the drive from Wales to Salisbury Plain, one of the guys lost control of the Land Rover he was driving and he died of his injuries. He was only 21 years of age but was already a big character in 79 Bty and 29 Cdo Regt. Will Priddy – who was nicknamed 'P Riddy' because of his love of rap music and a play on his name – was an extremely popular lad and his death rocked us all to the core. Gone but not forgotten Will, RIP.

The Property Portfolio Grows

It was also during this time that I decided that I wanted to buy another investment property and I was particularly interested in a place we could live as a family, but large enough so that Siân could have her own room and also allow us to rent the rest of the house out to others to create another income. We viewed a few places but nothing seemed to fit and it was actually my mum who spotted a house for sale in the local newspaper which I went on to buy and still own today. The house is a three-storey property on the Hoe in Plymouth, which had previously been used as a guest house called 'The Marion'. I raised the money for the deposit by re-mortgaging two of the flats I already owned. My plan was to create a downstairs flat for us and rooms that we could let out upstairs. There was already a little kitchen on the first floor and a bathroom and toilet on the first and second floors, so everything was in place. All I needed to do was refurbish the property as it was quite run down at the time. I didn't have enough money in the bank to do the refurb which cost about £25K and so I borrowed from credit cards to do it.

I'm not suggesting anyone does this, but the plan was to re-mortgage the property once the refurb was complete to pay off the credit cards. With hindsight, I would have to admit that I was fortunate that the UK housing market was still booming at the time (2005). So, once the house was refurbished, and also as a result of 'market appreciation', it valued up much higher: after re-mortgaging, I was able to pay off the credit cards and had enough money left over to buy a £10K car. This house was my first real taste of earning a significant extra income from property and it was also easy to manage in that we lived at the property as well.

Wedding Number 2

In the summer of 2005, we travelled to Vegas to get married. I had already been to America several times before but nothing I had previously seen was to prepare me for Las Vegas in terms of extravagance. One of the biggest shocks I had there was on the first day when checking into our hotel Circus Circus. I remember walking in the direction of our room after being given the key, and whilst walking I looked left through a large opening and saw a full size roller-coaster actually inside the hotel. This didn't fully register with me immediately and I remember walking for several seconds whilst trying to compute what I had just seen. I decided to walk back and take another look because I thought I must have been mistaken and so expected to see the theme park and roller coaster outside but no, it was definitely inside the hotel!

The wedding took place in the 'Little White Wedding Chapel' which was fun and we went to a nearby hotel for the reception afterwards. Quite a few family members were able to come too; on my side there was my mum and dad and Marion and David (sister and brother-in-law) and Siân was a bridesmaid. The next day we travelled by helicopter via the Grand Canyon to stay on a ranch for a couple of days. After getting back, one of the shows we saw was Tom Jones, which was also a great experience. Once back in the UK, we continued to improve the house and get it ready for paying guests, or at least I did when I wasn't away on exercise with the Army.

Back into Battle

Army life was to change dramatically for me the following year because we were 'warned off' for a deployment to Afghanistan. It was at this time that Jim was posted to 7 Para RHA, who would be deploying there before 29 Cdo Regt, and it was during our pre-tour training that we got the news that Jim had been killed in a firefight with the Taliban near a place called Forward Operating Base (FOB) Robinson in Helmand Province. I was absolutely gutted by this news and it also filled me with an immense feeling of foreboding about our impending deployment to Afghanistan. Jim was the first British soldier to be killed over there and many of us went to his funeral in his hometown of St Albans just before deploying there ourselves. This was the starkest reminder possible that we were going to a very dangerous place and that some of us might not come home again to our families. The only thing to do was to take a deep breath and get on with it, because that's what you'd signed up for and there was no turning back.

After the funeral we continued with our pre-tour training to deploy to Afghanistan ourselves, but now the training took on a whole new significance and I could see that everyone was taking it very seriously indeed. We arrived in Afghanistan in October 2006, landing in Kabul before flying by C130 Hercules to Camp Bastion in Helmand province, which is the main holding area for troops to deploy from to the smaller outposts. We then started the two-week process of taking over from 7 Para RHA and 'relieving them in place' at the various outposts throughout the Area of Operations (AO). Camp Bastion was a very well-defended place and there was very little enemy threat there because it was literally in the middle of nowhere and any enemy approaching could be seen for miles, so after a day or two you began to feel pretty safe. The food was good and the tented accommodation was comfortable with good access to toilets and showers. In fact, Camp Bastion was given the nickname 'Slipper City' a little jealously by the lads who didn't get to stay there much! I was sharing a tent with Mark, who was the BSM and Mick from 7 Bty who had also recently been promoted to Sergeant Major. Mick had mellowed somewhat since I had been in 7 Bty, which was probably because he was due to leave the Army the following year, and we got on a lot better this time around.

Before I could get too comfortable in Bastion, I was told that in a couple of days I would be deploying as part of a troop to a Forward Operating base near a Place called Sangin nicknamed Fob Robinson (Fob Rob), which is the place where Jim was living and working when he was killed. I must admit that it was a bit of a shock to be told this was where I would go first out of the dozens of possible places to go, and I couldn't help feeling nervous because this place, more than any other in Afghanistan for me spelled danger. The time to go came along soon enough and myself and about ten other guys were taken to the airstrip near the camp, where we would be taken by Chinook Helicopter (Helo) to Fob Rob. The other 12 members of the troop were going there by vehicle convoy.

I remember looking around at the other guys (who were mostly young lads in their early to mid-20s) and there were some very apprehensive faces, that's for sure. I am not sure how I looked but I did my best to be as calm and reassuring as I could. As I was the most senior guy in the group, I knew it was important for me to set an example. The Chinook is a large helicopter with two rotor blades and has a ramp at the rear to allow easy access for both troops and stores. After going through a sort of departure process from Bastion, we walked with all our heavy kit and equipment to the place where we would wait to be called forward onto the aircraft, which was being prepared prior to us getting on board. The airstrip is a very noisy and dusty place with a lot of rotor and fixed-wing aircraft coming and going at regular intervals, so I kept an eye on the tailgate of our Chinook for the signal for us all to get on.

As soon as the aircrew gave us the signal, we grabbed our heavy kit and equipment and weapons and made our way onto the back of the helicopter. It was at this point that I recognised the RAF guy who was manning the General-Purpose Machine Gun (GPMG) which was mounted on the rear ramp of the aircraft. Craig had been on my first Commando course, but he had been in the Royal Military Police (RMP) whilst on the course. We had a brief catch up over the engine noise until it was time to go, then he went about his business on board and I took my seat with the lads. The journey time was about 20 minutes long and as we set off, I was feeling a mixture of apprehension and excitement as I watched Camp Bastion grow ever smaller behind us. About ten minutes into the journey, Craig approached me and shouted into my ear that our vehicle convoy was under attack as it entered Fob Rob and a firefight was currently taking place there. I expected him to say that because of this we would be turning back because a Chinook is a big 'bullet catcher' and it would be too risky to land whilst a firefight was taking place nearby, but he told me we were still going in!

Now, I was really nervous because I had no idea what situation we would be getting into after getting off the helo. My mind was racing and I couldn't help thinking that Les, Welly and Ian had been killed in a very similar helicopter to this one on their initial insertion into Iraq – and here we were on our initial insertion, approaching a firefight currently taking place. I wondered briefly about not informing the other lads about the situation on the ground because the most likely scenario was that we would land, get off and everything would be fine. But I decided that just in case I needed them to immediately get involved in the firefight, I should tell them what was happening. As each man told the man next to him, I could see their eyes open a lot wider once the penny dropped, which was fascinating to watch because they were no doubt experiencing the same rush of emotions I had just had.

So, together we now approached this heightened danger with a feeling of excitement but also fear. The fear is largely due to not being in charge of your own destiny and being at the mercy of things outside of your control, such as the reliability of the aircraft, the skill of the pilot, and not least the accuracy of the enemy who would surely be firing at such an inviting target as the huge helicopter we were sitting in. I realised then that this was what being in a proper war must feel like: it was the first time I had felt like this in my Army career.

Craig gave us the two-minute, followed by the one-minute warning to land. I could see out of the windows that we were approaching a fortified position and there was a lot of activity going on below. But as we got closer to the ground, the view out of the windows became completely obscured by the dust that was being thrown up by the downwash of rotor blades when landing in this type of terrain. We landed with quite a bump and the rear ramp descended immediately and we got off with our kit as quickly as we could to allow the aircraft to take off again, because in this situation the pilot does not want to hang around for any longer than is necessary. We went to ground to the rear of the aircraft totally blinded by the dust and waited for it to take off, which it did a few seconds later. As the dust gradually subsided, the ability to hear what was going on around us returned sooner than our vision and it was the noise that gave me the biggest scare. I could hear the distinctive sound of British weapons firing which sounded very close, but inconceivably I could also hear the sounds of foreign, Russian-made (Taliban) weapons as well, which sounded just as close, if not closer. Even more bewildering was that I could hear the sound of British weapons coming from one side of us, but foreign weapons coming from the other, placing us directly in the middle. I was seriously shitting myself at this point and it wasn't until the dust cleared a little that I could see that the foreign weapons were actually firing away from us at the Taliban and I realised that the owners of these weapons were Afghan National Army (ANA) soldiers who were on our side and were busy firing outwards to keep the Taliban heads down whilst the helicopter landed and took off.

The layout of Fob Rob meant that the ANA formed the outer perimeter on this side of the camp and our guys manned the inner, with the helicopter landing site situated directly in between – placing us in the middle of the different weapons being fired. The relief I felt at this point was immense and it was only now that my heart rate began to settle down to a level approaching normal. One of the outgoing 7 Para RHA guys came over and introduced himself before taking us inside the compound and showing us around. A few minutes later, the convoy led by Lieutenant (Lt) Horne arrived unscathed after their contact with the enemy, so thankfully the whole troop of 23 had now arrived in one piece.

After the initial excitement of our insertion into Fob Rob, things did settle down a lot and, over the next few days, the 7 para RHA guys were taken back to Bastion to start their journey home to the UK. As soon as the place properly belonged to us, we set about making some changes to the layout and running of the camp to suit us better. Lt Horne, who was nicknamed Flipper because of his huge feet, and I were the most senior guys in the troop and between us we made all of the decisions affecting the 21 other 29 Cdo guys in Fob Rob. Our job was primarily to defend the camp and to man our two 105mm Artillery guns (Light guns), which would provide Artillery cover out to 17 kilometres (km) from Fob Rob in any direction.

My 'band of brothers'

We also shared the camp with guys from various other Army and Royal Marine units, who were there to specifically liaise with and train the ANA soldiers who were located on the other side of the HLS. The man in charge of these guys was a young DE captain called Tom. Tom was an Artillery Officer, but he had applied to come to 29 Cdo Regt and was due to go on his Cdo Cse after this tour of Afghanistan. I liked him immediately and I hoped that he would go on to pass the course and join the Regiment. He was very skinny and pale at the time, with a shock of ginger hair, and he would sometimes be on the receiving end of banter from the lads, especially when we learned that he wanted to become part of our Regiment. What didn't help his cause was that he was trying in vain to grow a beard because he thought it would make him look more authoritative, even though the ANA told him it was embarrassing and that he should shave it off. When he was able to train, he would do laps around the internal perimeter of the camp (which was about 400 meters) and as he went past, we would do mock 'sighting reports' on the radio of a man-sized pepperami in phys kit (running/training kit) inside the wire. After flicking us the bird, someone would always say, "What's the matter: too spicy for ya?" I am glad to say that after the tour, Tom did go on to pass the Cdo Course and went on to serve in 7 Bty and became a very well-respected officer in the Regiment.

Climbing the Afghan Ladder

One of the main changes I decided to make was to build another sentry point, which was a little controversial and not popular with all of the lads. I felt that we were vulnerable to an attack from the main entrance to the compound, as the ANA soldiers were guarding the entrance and they were just not trustworthy in my opinion. I watched them on a few occasions at night-time and they did not seem to be keeping a proper watch or sentry routine. In fact, during the day a man who claimed to be from the nearby village simply walked into the compound through the main gate unchallenged by the ANA soldiers. This was the last straw, and I decided that we would have to guard the entrance ourselves. This was a tough decision because there were only 23 of us and we already had to guard another sentry point. It wasn't a very popular decision with some because it added significantly to the workload, but I had to trust my instincts that it was the right thing to do and insist. For all I knew, the Taliban could have sent the man in on a recce to see where we were most vulnerable to attack. My concerns about the competence of the ANA sentry were soon confirmed in an incident where myself and Cristal – the lad I was 'stagging on' (on guard) with – could have been killed in the middle of the night. We were observing our arcs (keeping watch), when suddenly an automatic weapon opened up 30-40 metres away from our position. Rounds were pinging and ricocheting all around us and we both instinctively hit the deck behind the safety of the Hesco Bastion and sandbags. This was a real shock and it took a good few seconds for me to gather my senses and try to work out what had just happened because it didn't make sense.

The information that my brain had just received was that there was a single shooter between the ANA sentry point and our location, firing in our direction. Cristal and I gave each other the nod to get into position to return fire, which meant re-exposing our heads and shoulders to the danger. I have to admit it did require a bit of a deep breath because all of your instincts tell you to stay safe behind cover. Once we got above the sandbags and in a firing position, with us about to engage him, the shooter was now in plain view about 15 metres away. But even with adrenalin rushing through our veins, something stopped Cristal and I from opening fire. Again, what we were seeing just did not make sense. The shooter now had his weapon by his side and was looking down at the ground in between him and us, kicking at the deck. With my weapon still trained on him, it dawned on me that he was an ANA soldier. I then realised that he was looking at the ground, maybe for an animal that he had just opened up at, on full automatic, risking killing myself and Cristal. I lowered my weapon, and for a moment I was speechless and stunned, because I knew I had come within a split second of killing this man! The only conclusion that I arrived at to explain his actions was that he was high on drugs, which I'm sorry to say was commonplace at the time with some of the ANA. I went from feeling shocked and stunned, to extremely angry, in a couple of seconds. He probably couldn't understand the specific words I used, but I gave him one of the biggest bollockings I have ever issued. I'm sure he got the gist of how I felt about what he had just done! With the sound of my anger ringing in his ears, he shuffled off back to his sentry point in a bit of daze.

A couple of weeks later, another incident happened at Fob Rob where an ANA soldier killed one of his own unit during an argument. He went to shoot the guy he was arguing with, and the man about to be shot pushed the rifle barrel to one side just as the trigger was being pulled, so that a man who was observing the argument was unintentionally shot several times in the chest and abdomen. He was stretchered into our sick bay for our medics to try and save, but he died of his injuries. I remember seeing some of our young guys who were on hand to help coming back covered in his blood and pale with shock from what they had just seen.

These incidents had a profound effect on me as they made me realise that my life could be taken from me at any moment by the enemy or even by an idiot ANA member. As a soldier you can cope with the thought of being killed by the enemy, but what you can't come to terms with is the thought of being killed by your own side in such ridiculous circumstances.

At least now that the extra Sanger was in place I could relax more, certainly at night time when the majority of us would be sleeping, because I knew our guys were manning the entrance to camp and not relying solely on the ANA sentry point any more. We were able to settle into a camp routine that would every now and then be interrupted by the Taliban attacking us. These attacks were quite scary at first, although after a while they became almost normal events. Often, we would just return fire using our own small arms and 50-calibre machine guns and, on occasion, we would use our artillery guns in either indirect fire (taking out firing points at a distance) or direct fire (close range). These mini-battles we would have were often very exciting and would certainly break up the monotony of war which could be very boring because we were just waiting day after day for something to happen.

The main vantage point we had available to us was the highest rooftop in the camp. Two of the lads, called Benny and Q, worked from there most days. They were fire support team members whose main job it was to bring in indirect fire from artillery and mortars. They would also bring down fire onto the enemy with jets and attack helicopters like the Apache. The chain of command at Camp Bastion decided that I should help Benny and Q make some of the life-and-death decisions that they were being forced to make on their own. So, each time we were attacked I was now required to join them on the rooftop to help them co-ordinate the defence of Fob Rob.

The only way to gain access to the rooftop was via a rickety old ladder attached to the outside of the building. I can remember climbing this ladder during quiet spells in camp and feeling quite vulnerable because of being so exposed to potential enemy sniper fire, so having to climb the ladder whilst we were under attack suddenly took on a whole new level of risk.

Whenever the camp was under attack, you could hear the rounds whizzing past overhead, but when you're at the bottom of the ladder they're unlikely to hit you. When you're at the bottom contemplating climbing it, you know that you're significantly increasing the likelihood that you'll be hit by one of the rounds. You then have to consider the likelihood that the enemy will see you climbing the ladder and direct their attention and their fire at you, which makes it an even less appealing proposition, but maybe, just maybe, my presence on the rooftop would prove to be instrumental in saving life.

Each time I climbed the ladder, the adrenalin was helping me scale it at an impressive speed, bearing in mind the kit and equipment I was carrying. I don't know whether the sound of the rounds passing nearby were any closer to me, or if my heightened senses just made them feel nearer. It's an odd thing to think but I did not want one of these bullets, that cost just a penny to buy, to take my life away at any second. The fact that I could hear each one passing meant that I had escaped death on that occasion; I knew it was the one that I *didn't* hear that could bring about my end. All I knew is that I was tensing my entire body as I scrambled up the ladder because I thought that maybe that could lessen the damage done by a direct hit. At the top of the ladder, I was able to fall over the sandbag protection around the top of the rooftop and would land in a bit of a heap because to take any more time over it was not on the agenda. I would lie there for a second or two, catching my breath but also calming myself down a bit after a scary few seconds of activity. I must admit that on occasion I did contemplate asking one of the other lads to climb the ladder, but if anything had happened to them I would not have been able to live with myself, so I never did. It was my ladder to climb.

Coming Under Fire

One of the dichotomies of being in a combat situation is that when you are targeted by indirect fire, such as mortar or Chinese rockets, the immediate action is to take cover in the safest place available to you. But almost immediately as an artillery unit, you have to man your equipment in order to return fire – even though to do so means leaving your shelter and putting yourself in mortal danger. One time when we were being mortared and I gave the command to take cover, not long afterwards the order of "fire mission" came from the command post, which required everybody to assume their positions in action. Being out in the open and manning the guns whilst mortars are landing close by and not running for the safety of the shelters is a very surreal thing to make yourself do, because any one of those subsequent mortars could land directly on top of you. On one such occasion, I noticed that one of the gun numbers was not present whilst orders were coming from the CP to return fire. I ran back to one of the shelters where I had last seen him to check if he was still in there and I found him inside with a look of terror on his face. I felt a lot of sympathy for him because, after all, it was a scary thing to expect somebody to do. I could understand why he was so reluctant to leave the shelter, but this is the job that we all signed up to do and there was no way I was going to let him stay there whilst he was needed by his men. Returning fire on the enemy in itself could save lives which is why you are not afforded the luxury of remaining in safety under those circumstances. The bottom line is: no matter what is going on at the time when the command "fire mission" is given, you man the guns and return fire. I told him in no uncertain terms that he was to get his arse outside immediately and man that gun – and, to his credit, he did as he was told. That was one of the few times during my whole army career when I had to exercise my authority over someone and order them to put their life in significant danger. I'm glad I didn't have to do it often.

Getting Accustomed to a War Zone

I'm happy to say that during my time at Fob Rob, no one from our side was injured or killed despite the fact that the Taliban attacked us many times. My feelings of contempt toward the Taliban actually lessened during this time. I know that many of them were killed during the firefights that took place. Although I know that they are murderous and cruel in nature, I have learnt that they are by and large, poorly educated and indoctrinated pawns who are no match for our equipment. Meanwhile, their puppet masters and financiers sit in faraway places in the lap of luxury and complete safety. So, most of my contempt is reserved for those people.

After about six weeks in Fob Rob, I was told that I would be joining a different troop in the Battery that would be located further south in Helmand Province. This troop was already operating 'out on the ground' in a mobile role as opposed to being static in a fortified position. I was taken by helicopter back to Camp Bastion where I would spend a few days before re-deploying with my new troop. It was nice to be back in Bastion for a short time because the food was better, and the accommodation and facilities in general were good. It was also a lot easier to phone home and write emails!

The officer commanding this troop was Elliot, who I got on with well. My friend Sarse was also deployed to this troop, so I was looking forward to this next phase. We would be travelling south by vehicle to join the Mobile Outreach Group (MOG), which was essentially a convoy of vehicles containing soldiers and equipment. The main firepower within the MOG were the two 105 mm Light Guns which would provide fire support in and around the Garmsir area for any coalition units that might require it. The advantage of the MOG was that unlike somewhere like Fob Rob, where the guns were static, the MOG could be moved around to provide fire support in advance of a planned operation. This would be my first time outside of the protective confines of a fortified camp (apart from helicopter moves) and the prospect of going 'out on the ground' was a little daunting I have to admit.

Before I could get too comfortable in Bastion, the day arrived soon enough for me to leave again. Once all the vehicles were loaded, we set off on the long journey south. I was initially a little nervous going outside the wire but I began to relax once into the journey, probably due to the fact that nothing bad had happened. The reality was that for the vast majority of the time when travelling by vehicle in Afghanistan it was an uneventful experience, but it was the odd dangerous event which dictated that 100 per cent vigilance was required at all times and so you did not relax too much.

We arrived at the MOG some hours later and it was nice to see Sarse and Elliot again. The next day, the guys who we were 'relieving' set off in their vehicles back to Camp Bastion, where they would probably spend a few days before deploying to somewhere else within Helmand. When the MOG was static, all of the vehicles arranged themselves in a defensive set-up. The larger vehicles carrying the heavy machine guns would form the outer cordon, with the command and recce vehicles located towards the centre. The Artillery guns in the MOG will always have a Center of Arc (direction of most likely enemy threat) at any location, so once they are in place the rest of the vehicles are positioned to provide as good a defense of the position as possible.

Operating out on the ground in the middle of nowhere does take a little bit of getting used to, but after a while when nothing bad has happened it becomes almost normal and you settle down into a routine in which you don't feel too on edge, although never completely relaxed for obvious reasons. As is often the case during operations, life can get monotonous because for the vast majority of time, nothing is happening and you are just waiting for something to happen. It can be very boring. One of the aspects of modern warfare which is a bit weird is that when you're out on the ground, you carry a couple of satellite phones with you. The phones we had were like the big bricks mobile phones that first came out in the 80s. Each bloke was allocated 20 minutes of talk time a week free, although this was later increased to 30 minutes, and anything above your allowance had to be paid for. Each guy would set up an account with the phone service provider, called Paradigm, and any call charges over and above your free minutes would be paid for by direct debit. Life could get a bit monotonous in the MOG but one thing that would relieve the boredom was the requirement to go on reconnaissance tasks, which could often be required before deciding on the next gun/MOG position to occupy.

Elliot and I would go on the recce with one or two other vehicles and, due to the lack of numbers, this was when we were most alert. We tried not to use the same routes and tracks as much as possible because we knew that this would create a pattern that the Taliban could target with either an ambush, or more likely an IED. Our recces proved to be uneventful, which has a habit of lulling you into a false sense of security because, inevitably, you begin to believe that the Taliban must not be interested in taking you on and that they have bigger fish to fry elsewhere. We knew that there was plenty of Taliban activity in and around Garmsir because of the numerous artillery fire missions we would be engaged upon, but the action all seemed pretty far away to me.

After a few more weeks we would be 'relieved in place' by another troop, which was manned by 7 Bty guys and commanded by Lt Tim Rushmere who was another well-liked and respected young officer in the Regiment. Once the handover/takeover was complete, we made the long drive back to Camp Bastion. This was eagerly anticipated by us all because it meant fresh rations, a hot shower, some clean clothes and a comfortable bed! I was able to speak to my family as well as write some letters home, which was nice.

Christmas in Camp Bastion

The decision had been made that I would not be deploying back out from Bastion straight away as there was a lot of work to be done from there. There is still a lot of administrative work to be done even on operations. My job as the Training Warrant Officer required me to plan which career courses each man needed to attend and when he could do them. This required a lot of coordination with different people, departments and training establishments back in the UK. Another aspect of modern warfare is that during a six-month deployment, you are usually able to get two weeks R&R to get home.

The R&R cycle was also now in full flow which meant that individuals would go home for a couple of weeks, and this required people to cover other people's jobs whilst they were away.

I covered for the BSM of 79 Bty and the Battery Captain (BK). Both roles were not too difficult for me to cover whilst they were away because their systems and processes were easy to follow which was a relief! It is always a bit of a lottery regarding when you are allocated your R&R. You can ask for certain dates that are important, but there is no guarantee. I chose early February to try to coincide with Siân's and my birthdays and, luckily, I was allocated that time. Some guys are lucky enough to be allocated Christmas and/or New Year slots, but the flip side to that is it's a lot harder for you and your family to re-deploy to somewhere like Afghanistan immediately after spending such a special time with your family!

For the majority who are on operations over Christmas, the main event, which separates Christmas Day from any other day, is that the chefs (if you are lucky enough to have your food cooked for you) will make a special effort and do a really good Christmas dinner with all the trimmings. The festivities often involve a food fight, which does not go down too well with the poor kitchen staff as it all has to be cleaned up again afterwards!

It's easy to forget at times – like when wearing your Santa hat at the dinner table – that you are still in a war zone. On December 27, we were given the starkest reminder possible of this when one of the guys in 7 Bty was killed when the vehicle he was driving, as part of MOG South, struck an anti-tank mine near Garmsir. He was only 22 years old. It became clear that the Taliban had indeed targeted our vehicles that were moving around the MOG South area and the landmine was placed where our ISAF (International Security Assistance Force) vehicles were known to go. The incident was particularly difficult for the surviving guys who were also travelling in the Land Rover he was driving. The vehicle had been blown into the air and came to rest on top of the young lad trapping his leg. He was still alive at this point and the other guys were frantically trying to free him because the vehicle was on fire and the ammunition on board was heating up and exploding. The guys were actually getting burnt as they tried in vain to free him until eventually the fire forced them back. The postmortem concluded that he had already been fatally injured by the initial explosion, but it must have been horrendous for the lads to not be able to pull him away from the stricken vehicle at the time. I know that they have all suffered and found it hard to come to terms with what they witnessed and experienced that day, and I can only guess at how awful it must have been for them. This was the first fatality that 29 Cdo had experienced on this tour and it was a terrible shock for the Regiment. The men of 7 Bty continued to operate stoically and with utmost professionalism in the aftermath of losing one of our lads in such a terrible way.

A few weeks later 7 Bty returned to Camp Bastion and I gathered the men together to tell them how proud we all were of them and how they had conducted themselves. I found it really hard to keep my emotions in check as I spoke because as I was talking, I could see the turmoil in some of their eyes, and some of them were barely 20 years old. I then told them that they would be spending a few days in Bastion before deploying back out again for their next rotation.

A Brief Respite

Modern warfare is strange. New technology means for most of the time you are able to call your family from a war zone. I remember calling my wife and Siân after speaking to the 7 Bty lads because I had told them when I would call next, but I didn't want to call until I was feeling more in control of my emotions. The problem was that if I didn't call, they would be worried and so I just had to do it. They would tell me about their lives and struggles back home and I would do my best to be supportive and understanding but I know I was often distant and maybe a little grumpy. The problem is you don't want to talk about the sad or scary things happening to you because you don't want them to worry too much, and so the slightly awkward phone calls repeated themselves far too often.

I mentioned earlier about R&R, which is such a weird thing with modern warfare, because you are flying from a war zone and all that entails and literally hours later you are back home with your family in a safe and secure environment. The problem is that whilst on operations your brain is on a high state of alertness even when you are asleep, and to be able to switch this off immediately knowing that you will have to switch it back on again in a matter of days is just not possible. And so, you may be walking with your family to the cinema and you find yourself wondering if a Coke can with a twig sticking out of it in the street is an enemy marker for an improvised explosive device that is about to kill you and those around you. A car may screech around the corner and you are ready to bundle your loved ones into the a nearby hedge to protect them. It's lovely to be home with your family but it's a really hard thing to do at the same time because the clock is ticking as soon as you get home for when you have to go back to a war zone again. It's just as hard for your family in this respect because it's awful for them to have to welcome you home before waving you off again after a couple of weeks, which flies by. All this puts a big strain on the relationship you have with your loved ones, but especially your spouse. I managed to get home for my R&R in February, which coincided with Siân's birthday. My wife had organised a party for her and her friends and some of my family, which was a really nice evening. I did my best to relax that night and for the remainder of my R&R, but it was not easy, and after no time I was on my way back to Afghanistan.

Homecoming parade on returning from Afghanistan - me with Siân

Me with my Mum Kathy

Tragedy Strikes Again

It was now mid-February and there were only about six weeks of the tour left. Although there had been many casualties and fatalities affecting the other units we were deployed with (mainly Marines), thankfully no one else in 29 Cdo had been killed or injured. Tragically, this was about to change when the Taliban attacked one of our bases in Sangin. Two of our lads from 148 Bty were killed by a rocket attack. Again, this came as a huge shock to us all. They too were very young men who were best friends and they died together. If either of them had survived the other it would have been a huge loss to cope with, which is the only positive to draw out of this terrible tragedy.

They had been part of a four-man Fire Support Team and it was decided that the two remaining team members would be returned to

Camp Bastion for a short time to help them come to terms (as much as possible) with what had happened.

Another Fire Support Team would be flown in by helicopter to relieve them. This four-man team was led by Mick. Mick was a veteran of many operational deployments during his 22-year career but he said in our tent that he had a bad feeling about this one. Mark and I reassured him that after what had just happened, he was bound to be feeling uneasy and it would be fine. There is no way Mick would have shared this with his men, but as Mark and I were of a similar age and the same rank he didn't mind sharing his anxiety. Mick grabbed his kit and left the tent to go and meet up with his three other team members.

That was the last time I ever saw Mick. Only a few days later, he was killed in Sangin by a grenade attack in a firefight with the Taliban. This time, the shock that we all felt was off the scale. Mick was invincible. Nobody messed with him, and if they did they would regret it. There were only a few weeks remaining of the tour before going home to our families. Mick was due to leave the Army almost immediately after getting home. I don't know what Mick would have gone on to do with his life but it would have been something awesome, because he was awesome. He was, and will always be, a true legend of 29 Commando Regiment.

After a few more weeks, the advance party of the next battle group who would be taking over from us started to arrive. As was always the case, the outgoing troops briefed the incoming on everything from basic admin procedures through to advanced strategic planning. By strange coincidence, and also indicative of our ever-shrinking Army, my friend Gary (also at the rank of Sergeant Major) arrived in order to take over from me at the start of his six-month tour of Afghanistan. It was odd situation to be in, briefing

Gary on a professional level when he was my best friend. Being the guy that was going home, I felt relief and happiness, but etched on Gary's face at the beginning of his tour was the look of a man who had a hard and stressful six months ahead of him. It's difficult to reassure your mate that everything is going to be fine when we had just lost four guys from our regiment, including one at the same rank as us. All you can do is say, "best of luck" and "see you after the tour". Sadly, a sergeant from Gary's unit was killed during his tour, but thankfully Gary did get home safely.

Heading Home

This time, instead of flying straight home, we were taken to an Army camp in Cyprus. This was a new concept that the Army had introduced to allow the troops time to 'decompress' prior to arriving home from a warzone. There were lectures about how best to deal with the traumatic events that had taken place during the tour and how to ease yourself back into normal family life. There was also a BBQ on the beach with beer. A strict 'confined to camp' policy was in place because, for obvious reasons, the Army didn't want boozed-up squaddies hitting the tourist locations, still in a potentially volatile frame of mind, having literally the day before been in a combat zone. Decompression works well in that it lets the guys blow off steam and get some things out of their systems before getting on the final flight back to the UK.

Once back in Plymouth, there followed a few days' worth of admin in camp prior to going on post-operational tour leave. As opposed to mid-tour leave, this period of time is when you can properly switch off, relax and not stress about odd-looking coke cans and cars backfiring, and re-adjust to home life. Siân was now 14 and about to embark on her GCSEs. She continued to thrive at Plymouth

College, which was reassuring, and it was lovely to be able to spend some quality time with her during the weeks that followed.

Once back at work, I was informed that I was being promoted from Sergeant Major to Battery Sergeant Major of 148 Forward Operation Commando Battery Royal Artillery, based in Poole, Dorset. Whilst I was happy with this career progression, it did not go down too well at home because it would mean being away Monday to Friday as well as when on exercise and overseas. It's a typical example of the strain that is put on the marriages of service personnel, as it's not as straightforward as the family simply following the soldier where he/she is posted. My wife had a full-time job in Plymouth and Siân was settled and doing well in her school. So, I went to Poole on my own and commuted back to Plymouth at weekends. As a couple we endeavoured to make it work, but it was not easy and with hindsight, it weakened the marriage further.

I threw myself into my new job and worked very long hours as the BSM of 148 Battery with the knowledge that there was already another Afghanistan deployment scheduled in just over a year's time. Prior to that though, as well as several UK-based exercises, I also deployed to Norway (for six weeks), America and Gibraltar on various training exercises. In no time at all, it seemed, we were embarking on our pre-deployment (to Afghanistan) training again, which would commence in October 2009. The time passed very quickly and I was again saying goodbye to my family whilst promising them that everything would be fine and I would be ok. It was a hollow reassurance because everyone concerned knew that on my previous tour, four of 29 Cdo were killed, including Mick, who was the same rank as me and who I had shared a tent with.

Me with the guys about to parachute into the sea

Second Tour of Afghanistan

This time in Afghanistan, I was mainly based in Lashkargah which was the Brigade HQ location. As you would expect with an HQ, it was not as exposed as somewhere like Fob Rob and so we were not attacked as often. I think during the six months, we came under fire five or six times with mortar and rocket attacks. Some of the impacts came pretty close to exploding on top of our guys but, luckily, all of the attacks whilst I was there did not injure any of our people.

We had a weapon-locating radar system in the camp which will track the trajectory of the incoming rockets and mortars and plot the location of the firing point, and we did indeed positively identify (PID) the firing point during each attack. Under normal circumstances, we would have returned fire immediately on the firing point. But the location of the firing point caused us to hesitate, as when we cross referenced it to make sure that there were no friendly troops or civilians in that area, we discovered that the Afghan National Police (ANP) were logged as being in that exact place. The ANP were clearly on our side, trained by us, and employed by the Afghan Government, so we could not fire on a 'friendly' location if there was any doubt that our equipment was malfunctioning and giving us the wrong location of the firing point that was attacking us. One of the assets at our disposal was weaponised unmanned air vehicles (UAV) – or drones as they have become known – which also have a live feed video capability that we were able to watch real time back at the HQ. During one of the attacks, we PID'd the firing point which once again was listed as an ANP location, so we sent the UAV to that location to get the live feed. The video footage was conclusive: we could see a mortar detachment firing from the point in question, and these mortars were being fired at us and landing in and around our camp. Any one of these mortar rounds could have caused severe loss of life if one of them landed close to our troops or the civilians living just outside of our camp, so we gave the order for the UAV to engage the firing point. The UAV was armed with Hellfire missiles which are effective against armoured vehicles and so the mortar team who were not mounted in an armoured vehicle would have very little chance in the event of a direct hit.

Another surreal aspect of modern warfare is that you can often see a live feed of everything that is going on using the cameras mounted on our manned coalition aircraft and unmanned (UAV) aircraft. In this case we could see the feed from the camera mounted on board the UAV. In the seconds before impact, we watched as the Taliban mortar team frantically engaged in the activity of sending mortars on their way towards us, before the camera flare signifying the impact of the Hellfire. It was a direct hit and once the camera feed returned, we could see that the target had been 'neutralised'. The scene was now transformed in that there was no activity to be seen, but it was still possible to see bodies and equipment now displaced from where it/they had previously been. This also corresponded with no more mortar rounds landing in and around our location. There was a slight delay in this happening, due to the 'time of flight' of a mortar round but subsequently the incoming fire ceased at our location.

The next day we sent out a patrol to investigate the firing point and we discovered that the dead mortar team were indeed wearing Afghan National Police uniforms and were situated at an Afghan National Police location. This was truly a situation where you didn't know your friends from your enemies.

Working in the Brigade HQ was also surreal in that you were following in real time all of the operations taking place around the AO. One such operation was on the 14 January. Captain Tom, who I wrote about earlier on in my first tour of Afghanistan in Fob Rob, was on a roof top commanding a fire support team in support of an operation clearing Taliban compounds near a town called Gereshk. Tragically Tom was killed by 'friendly fire' when a Danish unit mistook his position for an enemy firing point and engaged with an anti-tank missile. Tom, I always had the utmost respect for you and you are sorely missed by all who knew you. RIP, my friend.

Once again, I faced the unnatural scenario where I was unable to go to Tom's funeral to pay my respects. But I was also unable to attend the repatriation ceremony at Camp Bastion where the coffin was carried on to the back of a C130 aircraft draped in the Union flag, which is a very emotional experience in itself but does allow a certain degree of closure and a chance to grieve and vent some of your emotions. I had to continue working in Lashkargah and could not go.

Yet another really weird aspect of modern warfare is the fact that normal routine admin has to continue and so I would spend a lot of my time writing confidential reports (in civilian life I believe the equivalent is an annual report or review) on people as well as arranging exercises and courses and adventure training for the men in the Bty to do once back to normal work in the UK. One minute you are doing routine paperwork and the next you are engaging enemy firing points using drones engaging with Hellfire missiles! Modern warfare is simply weird.

There was more tragic news to come when news arrived that another 29 Cdo officer had been killed in one of the Forward Operating Bases. Lieutenant Aaron Lewis was killed by enemy fire from such a distance that the guys in the FOB didn't even know they were being fired at. It was such an unlikely event that a 'pot shot' from such a distance would actually hit someone, but tragically for Aaron, one of these rounds found its mark and he was killed. One of the things I find hard to come to terms with is that a bullet in countries like Afghanistan cost about one penny to buy, but the impact that they make on people's lives cannot be measured. RIP Aaron, you are sorely missed by all who knew you.

The six-month tour continued to drag on monotonously, but I was able to get my mid-tour leave in again in February, so I was able to get back for Siân's 16th birthday. We hired a function room by the marina on the Barbican in Plymouth and Siân invited lots of her friends from school. We all had a lovely evening and tried not to think of the ticking clock which would see me return to Afghanistan in a few days.

At least I had 'broken the back' of the tour now and I would only have about six weeks to do by the time I got back out there.

Upon my return, I was given the news that after I had completed my Post Operational tour leave, I would be taking over as the Regimental Quartermaster Sergeant which is a logistics job. This is the most senior Sergeant Major appointment in the Regiment and it involves being the right hand man to the Quartermaster (QM) who is usually a late-entry Major who has previously been an RSM before becoming a Commissioned Officer. Its normally a role given to a Battery Sergeant Major who has not managed to be promoted to Regimental Sergeant Major (RSM). I was still eligible for promotion to RSM, so I hoped they weren't trying to tell me something with this appointment! This move also meant that I would have served as a Senior NCO (Sergeant to Sergeant Major) in all of the five Batteries of 29 Cdo Regt, which is very rare and something I am very proud of.

Career Success – What about Family?

I really didn't like logistics as it involved lots of paperwork, audit after audit, and stock check after stock check. The main benefit of this job however was that it involved being back in Plymouth again. This did help ease the strain on my marriage a little, but as is always the case as well as other trips away, I was soon preparing for a six-week deployment to Norway the following winter. We were now simply not getting on and we would frequently argue. When I went to Norway we were arguing – and the arguments continued whilst I was away. I even remember the silly thing that we were arguing about which was our Economy Seven heaters in the flat and whether they needed to be switched off at the wall during the day in order to save money on our electric bill. I knew that these heaters only use electricity during the night, so you could leave the switch in the 'on' position during the day instead of trying to remember to switch them on before going to bed at night (which is what my wife was insisting on). Inevitably, because we often didn't remember to do that, we would have a cold flat the following day. I decided, unwisely, to prove I was right by researching it whilst I was away and emailing the proof that I was right. Not my finest hour I have to admit, and it certainly didn't help! Not long after returning from Norway, I received the news that I had been successful on the promotion board and I would indeed be promoted to Warrant Officer Class One (WO1) as well as being awarded the appointment of Regimental Sergeant Major (RSM). This was a massive achievement for me as it's the highest rank you can get to as a soldier before becoming a Commissioned Officer. My dream of becoming a Commissioned Officer in 29 Cdo was now extremely likely because there were several 'Late Entry' posts in 29 Cdo to be filled, but there were not too many Cdo-trained men eligible to fill the posts. So as far as I was concerned, I was now within touching distance of achieving my career-long ambition.

The bad news for my marriage was that it involved moving away from Plymouth again. The job was in Luton which was where the Regimental HQ for 100 Regiment RA was based. It was soon after this news, and whilst I was still in Norway, that my wife asked me for a divorce and I agreed that it was for the best.

As well as going to Luton and commuting for the next two years, the other factor in play was that there was another Afghanistan tour for 29 Cdo scheduled in a couple of years' time. If I did indeed return to the Regiment as an officer, it was likely that soon afterwards, I would be going back there again. These are the strains that marriages are put under if you are in the military, and only the strongest of marriages can survive it. A full Army career for someone starting at the lowest rank (private equivalent) is 22 years long, but if you are one of the few who becomes a late-entry officer then your career can easily, and often does continue, until you are 55 years old. This is clearly a long time to be married to a soldier and although it wasn't nearly that long, my marriage was just not strong enough to endure any longer.

At this time, I had six properties which were flats and houses including a seven-bedroom HMO. I decided that I would sell three of the flats in order to create a lump sum for a divorce settlement. I agreed to give my wife a considerable amount of money to help her move on and have a decent deposit to put down on her next place.

The problem I faced with trying to sell the flats to create a divorce settlement was that this was 2010 and the country was in a deep recession. Property values had significantly dropped, so the flats were not selling at the price I needed to clear the existing mortgages and leave the lump sum I needed. I had overestimated how much equity was in my portfolio and I therefore offered far too large a divorce settlement. My wife had already offered on her next house to live in and was counting on the money from me, so I was in a very difficult position indeed. I had emptied the flats of tenants in order to sell them; I also spent a lot of money on decorating and new carpets. I was now paying all of the bills, as well as the mortgages, but getting no rent! I was getting further and further into debt and feeling pretty desperate. In the end, I decided to give up trying to sell the flats and borrowed the money instead to hand over as a divorce settlement. I rented the flats back out, so at least I stopped the haemorrhaging of money. But I was now left with a lot of debt to service!

Time to Move On

100 Regiment was a mixture of regular and territorial army (TA – also known as reservists) men and women, and it was a significant

change from only working with 'regular' commando-trained soldiers. What some people don't know is that TA soldiers will usually have a full-time job, so the level of commitment and enthusiasm will usually be less than that of a regular (full-time) soldier. Their level of training will usually be less too, which is completely understandable. This situation dictates that the way in which TA soldiers are managed needs to be more relaxed and a leader's expectations of them needs to be less, in that they won't always do what they are told when they are told, as a regular soldier will. I found this situation to be quite frustrating at first because I just wanted people to do what they were told, when they were told! The RSM of a regiment needs to have a good relationship with the Commanding Officer (CO) who is usually a Lieutenant Colonel, but as with any relationship this is not always easy. The first CO I encountered was a great guy who was very popular and well-liked by everyone in the Regiment and I got on really well with him. One reason for this was that he was not pushing hard to be promoted to full colonel which helped create a more relaxed atmosphere for all under his command.

If a CO is given a TA regiment to command, it is extremely unlikely that he will be able to promote to full colonel at the end of his tour. The reason is that all regiments will have a pecking order in terms of prestige and the TA regiments will be placed at the bottom of this order.

My first CO understood this, but he was replaced after a few months by a CO who definitely wanted to buck the trend. I felt that he was pushing everyone too hard in order to make a name for himself and to stand out from the crowd. The RSM is the bridge between the soldiers in a regiment and the CO, so I felt it was my duty to tell him this. He definitely did not agree with me, which caused us to clash throughout our working relationship, but I do not regret doing it.

It was a dilemma for me at the time because I wanted to be promoted at the end of my RSM tour and I needed a good report from him to stand a good change achieving that. One person in particular made my time at 100 Regiment a lot more bearable: that was Rob who was posted in shortly after I arrived as the Adjutant, who is a senior captain, and like me had to work closely with the CO. Rob was posted in from 29 Cdo Regt too and we had served together in Afghanistan which I think helped a lot.

Personal Happiness

Being posted to Luton was a bit lonely because I was now single and when not at work I would simply spend time in my flat alone. I wanted to meet someone but that's really hard to do when you are removed from your normal social circle, so I decided to give online dating a go. My previous success at meeting the right person hadn't gone too well, so why not! One of the reasons for choosing online dating to find a partner was to align our compatibility regarding the desire to have kids. Most of my adult life to this point had been dominated by being a father and the commitment – rightly so – that comes with that. Siân was now 17 years old and would soon be leaving school to go to university. Financially, this would ease the pressure on me considerably. Also, with Sian moving into adulthood, the father-daughter relationship would be more straightforward too. I decided that I did not really want to have any more kids with my next partner, but I knew that if I fell in love with someone who really did, I would probably agree to it. I would obviously then fall in love with the child too, which would be a life-changing event!

What worried me with the conventional way of meeting someone was that you could be with someone for years before finding out that the other person actually wanted kids, when you were initially under the impression that they weren't that bothered. You may have been clear from the outset that you didn't want kids, but they were hoping that you would change your mind! With online dating, you could read people's preferences on this in advance of contacting them, so I decided to only select women to contact who stated clearly that they did not want to have kids with a future partner. I was 39 years old and I only selected women who were a similar age to me, so it was easier to find women who had already had kids and didn't want any more or who had never had the desire to be a parent. I had a few dates over a couple of months, but without meeting anyone I liked or connected with. One woman would frequently tell me stories about all of the different men she would flirt with – from the guy in the car wash to Jeremy Clarkson when she was an audience member on Top Gear! There were other compatibility issues too, so I decided to call time on that. I am someone who is attracted to a strong, intelligent woman; someone who is perfectly capable of standing on her own two feet if necessary, but who wants to share the journey with someone emotionally.

In my earlier years, I didn't feel worthy enough to be with a person like that, but my self-confidence had gradually improved over time and now I was able to imagine myself with such a person.

When I saw Caroline's profile it really got my attention. She was three months younger than me, attractive, and very successful in her career. But was she too successful to be attracted to me? She was in a senior IT management role with a large global company. I was a soldier going through a divorce with a struggling property portfolio. I eventually plucked up the courage to reach out to Caroline and we started to communicate.

I was living on the outskirts of Luton at the time, in my Army-rented flat, and Caroline was living in St Albans which was a short drive away. Our first date was at the Halfway House in Dunstable, near Luton. I got there first, followed shortly after by Caroline who coincidentally parked her car right next to mine. I had a black Audi A5 coupe and she had a black Audi TT. The cars were definitely suited to each other, but would we be?

Caroline says that when she saw me waiting for her on the steps of the pub, she said to herself, "He'll do, so far," and I definitely felt the same way about her. We got on really well from the outset and there was definitely a strong connection between us. We were both from working class backgrounds which helped us to feel comfortable with each other. It impressed me a lot that Caroline had also left school at 16, but had achieved so much in her career. The two hours we spent together in the restaurant flew by and there was never an awkward moment. We made each other laugh as well as sharing common values. I was really keen to see Caroline again and thankfully she wanted to see me again too. Our relationship grew stronger and stronger and we became a couple. I soon fell in love with Caroline and I wanted to spend the rest of my life with her, but I could see trouble ahead which would very likely jeopardise our future together. The job I had in the Army at the time bore very little resemblance to the one I would return to in a year and a half. Now, I was able to meet Caroline after work and at weekends when I wasn't seeing Sian. But after my time in Luton, I would return to 29 Commando Regiment in Plymouth, which would be a 4.5 hour drive from St Albans. I would then go back to deploying overseas again, which would include operational deployments. In fact, 29 Commando were preparing for another Afghanistan deployment which would happen shortly after my return to the regiment.

I knew from experience the strain that normal Army life has on a relationship and it really worried me that my relationship with Caroline might not survive my return to the regular Army. We were a few months in to our relationship and I had still not mentioned what the future held for me. I just didn't know what to do for the best. My dilemma was that it was still my ambition to become a late-entry officer in my regiment, but I couldn't see a way of achieving that ambition and maintaining my relationship. Some people will ask, 'Didn't she know what she was getting involved in?' But the point is that no, she didn't know, because her experience of me being in the Army was completely different to the norm and she had no experience of military life. I continued to bury my head in the sand.

Property Investment Education

Caroline's mum and dad (Paul and Lesley) lived in Luton and we would often meet there after work. Paul had been given two free tickets to attend a property investment seminar and asked us if we wanted them. We said "yes" and went along not really knowing what to expect. The speakers shared their story and success in property investing and then offered further training that would need to be paid for. I had no idea there was such a thing as property investment training and I was very excited to learn more and Caroline was too. Over the years since then, we have spent tens of thousands of pounds on learning different property strategies and on mentors, and we still do that to this day. The point is: there is always more to learn and we know the power of having a mentor to advise us and keep us on track.

Once I started attending these courses, I got excited about how I could be building my property portfolio. I was hearing about how to raise funds for property investing: how to add value to property to be able to recycle that money back out when refinancing at its new higher value. How to create a lot more cashflow by investing in houses in multiple occupation (HMO) where tenants rent by the room. How property can be used for short-term rental to corporate and leisure guests to create a lot more cashflow than single lets. How to buy and sell houses to make lump sums of profit.

I got really excited by the lease purchasing strategy. That's when you can take control of a property on a lease without buying it, giving the owner the single-let rate each month, but you can use the property as an HMO or as serviced accommodation to generate cashflow. You can purchase the property at a later date once you have saved up the deposit funds. The purchase price is fixed at the time of entering into the option agreement.

Another exciting strategy was how you could rent someone's property at the single let rate but use it as serviced accommodation or an HMO to create lots of cashflow. This is not a 'how to' property book, but if you search for other books that I have written, you will be able to learn these property strategies in detail.

This was now October 2010 and the property education I was receiving, and the excitement it was creating in me, started to change my ambitions for the future because I could now see two paths ahead of me. One involved me pushing for a commission and returning to 29 Commando Regiment as an officer and continuing my Army career indefinitely, which would put a huge strain on my relationship. The other involved me building a property portfolio to a level that would get me out of debt and replace my job income but meant giving up on my Army ambitions. This would create a much better environment to be able to maintain my relationship. I decided that the Army had to go because I knew that my future happiness was at stake, but also I would never create great wealth in the Army. This was a seminal moment in my life.

The Journey to Financial Freedom

When I went back into work everything had changed, because I was now looking for the exit, not the next promotion. It used to be the case that you would hand in your notice using a paper form. Now it was an electronic form to be submitted. I sat at my desk for several days in a bit of a daze thinking, 'Am I really going to resign?' An RSM resigning is pretty unheard of. He or she will nearly always be trying for a commission or, at the very least, trying to stay in the Army for as long as possible. I would need to serve for one year from the date of giving my notice, but when should I do it?

A very significant date for most military people is Armistice Day or Remembrance Day which is the 11th of November each year. It marks the day World War One ended, at 11am on the 11th day of the 11th month, in 1918. This is when we remember 'the fallen' in that war and all wars since (Remembrance Sunday is the Sunday nearest to 11 Nov each year and so the date varies). Remembrance Day is a very important day for me (as it is for millions of people) because of the friends I knew who made the ultimate sacrifice, because they would never get to spend the rest of their lives with their loved ones. These are the immortal words that are read out prior to the 'Last Post' on Remembrance Day:

> *"They shall not grow old, as we that are left grow old.*
> *Age shall not weary them, nor the years condemn*
> *At the going down of the sun and in the morning*
> *We will remember them."*

I made the decision that I would hand in my notice on Remembrance Day, which means that I would be able to spend the rest of my life with my loved ones. This was simply a gesture from me and my way of saying 'thank you' to the fallen: "You gave your today for our tomorrow."

I also had another motive for choosing this day. For me to get myself out of debt and create enough passive income in one year, to be able to leave the Army without the need to get a job, was going to require hard work and sacrifice. They however had made the ultimate sacrifice. I concluded that if I failed in my task, I would not just be failing myself but failing them – and I <u>could not</u> let that happen.

I went into work on 11 November 2010, sat at my desk, and submitted my resignation, before going to St Thomas's Church in Stopsley in Luton for a Remembrance Day service to pay my respects at 11am. During the two-minute silence, I made a pledge to them that I would not fail and It was now my mission to leave the Army on 11/11/11 without the need to get a job.

Handing in my notice definitely got some attention from above. I would get phone calls from senior officers assuming that I had made an unintentional error on my computer. I had to explain several times that I had indeed done it on purpose! They would say things like, "But you could commission and have a job for life" and "Think of your pension, man!"

The ironic thing is that there is no such thing as a job for life. I had seen several of my Army friends and colleagues lose their jobs in the Army, as soon as they were injured or suffered from physical or mental illness.

A soldier gets a full pension after 22 years of 'man-service' (for which you must be 18 years and older). When it came to my pension, because I didn't start my two-year RSM's tour until I was 39, by the time I would leave the Army on 11/11/11, I would be past my 22 years of 'man-service' and therefore still get my pension. I explained this to my senior officers, but it only seemed to exasperate them further! They thought I was a fool to think that I could leave the Army early to be a full-time property investor and that I was making a big mistake.

The irony is that although they were much more senior in rank than me, on a much higher salary, with a much better conventional education, they were not qualified to give me financial advice. Don't get me wrong: their interventions were definitely making me very unsure of myself and the wisdom of my decision. After all, they didn't even know about the debt I was in due to the attempted property sales and divorce settlement. At the time, in 2010, the Army was in the process of reducing its number from 120,000 down to 80,000 and I was warned that there would be no turning back once my termination was final. One Colonel called me on the phone and said, "I have got your termination application in front of me on my computer screen. If I press 'enter' you will be leaving the Army next year. Or I can delete it and you can pretend it never happened – what would you like me to do?" I had to take several deep breaths at this point! After a prolonged period in which neither of us spoke, I said, "Sir, please press enter." He did, it was done, and the clock was now well and truly ticking!

Now that I was definitely leaving the Army, it was a very strange feeling. For the first time in my 23-year Army career, I did not actually care if my Commanding Officer disapproved of me! Under normal circumstance if that were the case, one would get a bad confidential report, and this would adversely affect promotion and therefore income and pension in the long run. It is a big dilemma for an RSM who wants promotion to be in, because his role is to act on behalf of the soldiers of the regiment and to disagree with the CO if he feels it is in the soldiers' best interests. The unusual situation that now presented itself was that of a CO of a TA regiment, who wanted to push the men hard in order to impress and gain promotion, and an RSM who had nothing to lose by pushing back and disagreeing with the CO. Needless to say, we clashed quite a lot. To cut a long story short, when it came to me getting my confidential report the CO wrote me a stinker – which is understandable based on the fact that we clashed so much! I had no intention of challenging it: I just wanted to sign it and leave his office. But before I left, he said, "You do understand that if you had wanted to stay in the Army and get a commission, this report would not have been good enough for you to do that don't you?" What would have infuriated him, I am sure, is that it did not upset me in the least.

The Commanding Officer of 29 Commando Regiment, Lt Colonel Smith, who I had served with for many years and have immense respect for, said in his last report of me, "I would have him as a late entry officer in 29 Commando Regiment tomorrow." That's all I needed to know.

When an RSM leaves the Army, it is traditional to have a 'dine out' which is a formal Regimental dinner night. It is customary for members of the regiment to contribute money or 'chip in' to create a pot of cash to buy a nice leaving present to go on the mantelpiece for ever more. The problem I had was that I couldn't bear the thought of spending the evening sitting next to the CO exchanging pleasantries (or not, potentially)! He would have to give a speech about me, and I would have to give an acceptance speech. He was chasing me to choose one of the potential days he had suggested, but I was stalling because I really didn't want a dine out with him there. In the end, he would not let me go without choosing a date. I still can't really believe I said the following, but I did: "Sir, I will have a regimental dine out as long as you are not there." He said, "Well, in that case you will not be having one," to which I replied, "Ok Sir, fair enough". He later came back to me and said "But what about your leaving presentation? The men have all contributed and it would be wrong for you to just accept the money." I said, "Sir, you are absolutely correct, that would not be right. Please donate the money to a military charity and please inform the men where their money went with my blessing." It wasn't the best way to finish my Army career and I do regret it finishing with such acrimony.

As I write, this happened nearly 10 years ago, and I have no ill feeling towards him whatsoever. This is just what happens when people clash in the workplace. The CO didn't get promoted at the end of his tour, but reaching the rank and position he did was a great achievement in itself and I commend him for that.

I have told this story because it was a very tumultuous and stressful time in my life and many people reading will have clashed and struggled with their own boss at work. I think it is good to know that it happens to many people. One of the reasons I share my trials and tribulations in the workplace is that most people earn their money in a job with a boss or bosses. Many people will not enjoy working for their boss and, to make matters worse, they may not like working with some of their colleagues either! A job can be an absolute thing of dread for many people and cause extreme anxiety and depression. But you don't have to earn your money in a job. A job is exchanging your time for money, or put differently, exchanging your life for money – and let's face it, some people risk their lives for money. Life can be very short, and it would be such a shame to literally lose years of your life whilst being unhappy in a job. I was now in my final year of having a job and my mission was to leave without the need to get one, so I needed to pull my finger out!

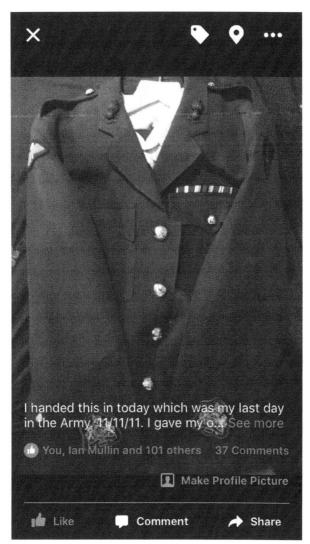

Saying goodbye to the uniform on
Remembrance Day on Social Media

Goodbye Soldier, Hello Property Entrepreneur

Growing the Portfolio Properly

The strategy that I knew the best was single-let property, so Caroline and I decided to focus on that. What we had learnt on our property training, was you can 'buy refurbish refinance' (BRR) property to pull your money back out – enabling you to go again and build a portfolio whilst recycling cash. To be able to do this, you need to buy a property below market value and/or add value to it by doing things like creating an extra bedroom or a parking space where the front garden was. Then, the property is worth significantly more than the price you paid for it, you can borrow against that new value and pull all or much of your money back out.

This strategy works particularly well in the parts of the country where property prices are relatively low. When a rental property is relatively cheap to buy, the gross yield on the property is high. The yield is the annual rent divided by the property value multiplied by 100 to make it a fraction. It's important to remember that most buy to let lenders will do a 75% loan to value (LTV) mortgage but they will only lend up to that figure if the rent for the property will cover the monthly mortgage payment with a decent margin on top, which could easily be 150% more, which is called the rental cover. So, at 150% rental cover if the monthly mortgage payment amount is £500, the rent would need to be £750 for the lender to lend up to 75% of the value of the property. If the maximum rent achievable per calendar month (PCM) was only £650, the lender would reduce the LTV to the level that would create a monthly mortgage payment that is 150% less than £650 which would be £433. The important thing to take into consideration when choosing an area to invest in, is: rents do not correspond to property values. Typically, the higher the property value, the lower the gross yield will be. At the time of writing, you can easily buy a property in some areas of the UK for £80,000 and rent it out for £500 PCM. That would be a 7.5% yield and the lender will easily lend you 75% LTV on that property because the rental mortgage cover is healthy. In a different area, you could buy a property for £200,000 but only be able to rent it out for £650 PCM. That would be a yield of 3.9%. Depending on typical mortgage interest rates at the time, the lender is unlikely to offer a 75% LTV because the rental mortgage cover would not be sufficient. This would mean you would need larger deposits for less overall rent, and you would be leaving bigger chunks of money in the properties post-refinance, making it a lot harder to recycle the money into subsequent properties. It would also be harder to raise money for property investing because the return on investment (ROI) would be low compared to what would be achievable in the cheaper areas.

Nutter Phone

By now I had moved in with Caroline in St Albans and property prices are high there, so we needed to choose elsewhere. I had lots of family in Swansea, including my dad who had built up his own property portfolio there, so it seemed the obvious place to choose. I had learnt that a really good way to get property below market value was to go 'direct to vendor' which means direct to the property owner and not via an estate agent. The traditional way of doing this is to drop leaflets through letterboxes. I decided not to go for that option as it would involve a lot more moving parts and costs for me in terms of getting the leaflets printed and distributed. Leaflets are more likely to work after someone has seen them multiple times, which can be a bit of a slow burn and I was in a rush!

I decided to go for an advert in the local newspaper called a 'goldmine ad'. The goldmine reference relates to the area you choose for your property investing. The newspaper I chose was the *South Wales Evening Post* which covers Swansea and the surrounding areas. Caroline and I got our heads together to come up with the advert which eventually read: 'Sell your property fast: call Kevin for a free valuation and a guaranteed offer!' We had been taught that it is best to put a woman's name on the advert as people are more likely to call a woman, but should I put Caroline's name on it? I was definitely going to be the person taking the calls, but I was meant to say, "Sorry, Caroline can't take your call at the moment, can I help?" However, the way I felt about that was it was starting the whole thing off on a lie and I didn't want to do that, so I kept it as Kevin. We were told not to use our personal phone number because people would be likely to call it at all times of the night and day.

The advice was to get a spare phone called a 'nutter phone' because from time to time nutters will call you on it! This phone could be turned off in the evening or during meetings at work, for instance. As Caroline was going into town one day, I asked her if she would pick up a cheap 'nutter phone' for me to use and she came back with a lilac one. So not only did I have to carry two phones around with me including at work, but I also had to speak to nutters from time to time and one of my phones was lilac!

The whole concept was that people would call you to invite you to make them an offer on their house or flat for sale. Clearly, we were in St Albans and Swansea was four hours away, so I would usually arrange the viewing to take place at the weekend if I could. On the odd occasion, if the vendor was really impatient, I would ask my dad to go around to the house to give me feedback on it. In some cases, I would make an offer in advance of seeing it if I couldn't get away from work to do it. This offer would be subject to us actually seeing the property, but it bought me some time. Needless to say, we were doing a lot of driving back and forward to Swansea during this time! As I said earlier, to make buy BRR work you more often than not have to secure a property at below market value, as well as adding value by means of a refurb and potentially things like an extra bedroom. Most of these below market value offers will be rejected, but if you are getting too many "yes" answers, you are probably offering too much money. In making your offer, you need to work backwards from what the property will be worth once you have completed your refurb. If you choose an area that has a lot of 'like for like' property (most cities fit that bill), you will be able to find comparable properties that have sold in good condition in the last couple of years that will provide a very good indication of what your prospective property will be worth when ready to sell or refinance. You work backwards from the end value, subtracting your costs and the equity that will be left in the property to arrive at the offer price. If the property will be worth £100,000, and the gross yield is good, you will get a mortgage on the property of £75,000 (£25K equity left in the property). If you are going to need to spend £15,000 on the refurb, you're now at £60,000. If your buying costs (such as taxes and legal fees) are £5,000, your offer price will need to be £55,000. The property in a poor condition might be worth £65,000, so you simply make your offer of £55,000. You buy the houses where the answer to your offer is "yes" and each "no" gets you one step closer to your next "yes".

In my experience, people do business with people they know, like and trust. I was confident enough at this point to go into people's homes, build rapport and work out win-win situations and I had a really good ratio of offers that resulted in a yes. Something that always surprises people when I tell them it, is that before making an offer on a property I always say, "You do know you would be able to get more than I can offer via an estate agent don't you?" If people accept my offer, it is usually down to time and they will say, "Yes, I know that Kev, but …"

They might not have time to sell via an estate agent, due to repossession proceedings or they might have found their dream home and they need to move really quickly or they will lose it. I think that the fact that I have said they could get more via an agent reassures them that I am honest will not try and rip them off. I had a situation once where the seller had been offered a higher amount from someone else who also had an ad in the newspaper, but she accepted our offer because she knew she could trust me. She was being repossessed and she couldn't risk the buyer dropping the offer price at the last minute to exploit the situation, which happens a lot unfortunately. The other offer was £2000 more than ours, but even though she had accepted our offer and wanted to proceed, I raised the offer by £2000 because that was a lot of money for her. Even though I might have left a couple of grand in the deal at the backend, it felt like the right thing to do. As it turned out, the property valued up much higher than expected, so we still got all our money back out post refinance. One lady even left a bouquet of flowers when she left the property because she had been able to move on and buy the home she really wanted due to the speed at which we could complete on the purchase of her property. I firmly believe that honesty pays, and you need to be able to look at yourself in the mirror and like and respect the person looking back at you. On occasion, when I have said, "You do know you could get more from an agent don't you," the seller has answered, "Oh right, fair enough: I will sell with an agent then!" You win some, you lose some I suppose.

When an offer would be accepted and we bought a house, we would then need to get it refurbished. To start with, my dad would help to oversee the refurb and manage the builders for us. Many of these builders were contacts of his that he had built up over the years. After a while, we created our own team of builders and one builder in particular who was good at project managing the whole job himself. We would be travelling back and forth from St Albans, mainly at the weekend, to make certain decisions and to oversee the projects. By now, we had several on the go at once being refurbished. Most were destined to be refinanced and kept, but some we sold on to create lump sums to help me get out of debt. The ones we sold on were the ones that wouldn't yield very well. These were the higher value properties that:

A. Wouldn't cashflow that well because the monthly mortgage payment would be high and the rent would not be that much more.

B. Would have a comparatively large chunk of equity left in it, so the cashflow would represent a low return on that equity.

There is a lot more rental demand for the cheaper-to-rent properties in any town and therefore the void periods are much less in between tenants.

Remember that due to the goldmine ad, I wasn't selecting properties to go and view to make offers on: people were inviting me to make an offer on a wide variety of property. I would make a BRR offer if it would work well to keep as a BTL and a buy-refurbish-sell offer if it wouldn't work well as a BTL.

Using Other People's Money

The reason we had several projects on the go at any one time was because we were using private investors' money to use for deposits and for the refurbs. When a property either sold or was refinanced, the money was either repaid with interest or it was used again on the next house. We have had very little problem raising money for property investing over the years. People invest with people they know, like and trust too!

To date, we have raised hundreds of thousands of pounds in private finance from friends and family as well as from friends of friends who we have never even met by just doing a straightforward loan agreement detailing the terms of the loan. We have learnt that when you are able to give people a much better rate of return than they are getting in the bank, you will be able to raise private finance. People often come forward with money to invest, which is a surprise because I would never have expected them to have a pot of cash to invest. The reason for this is most people with money to invest don't make a lot of noise about it because they would soon have people knocking on their door wanting to borrow it interest free, with very little chance of paying it back!

Remembrance Day 11/11/11

It was hard work and pretty stressful in the year after handing in my notice but I did indeed achieve my mission. A phrase I love is: if something is important enough you will find a way; if not, you will find an excuse. There were two things that were really motivating me during that year. The first was the desire to never have a boss again and to be the master of my own destiny. By not having a job, and having enough recurring income from property, you can do what you want, when you want, with whom you want. That to me represents complete freedom. The second was the pledge I had made exactly one year earlier in the Stopsley Church to my fallen comrades because by failing I would not just be letting myself down, I would be letting them down which would have been inexcusable. Failure was just not an option.

In the year after handing in my notice, I added another six properties to my portfolio, bringing the total to twelve. Caroline added a similar number to her own portfolio. I still had some debt to clear but it was manageable. Now that I no longer had a job, I was able to concentrate on building my property portfolio at pace. Not long after I had stopped working in a job, Caroline decided she wanted to be a full-time property investor too and left her job in 2012. We decided to move to Swansea to concentrate on building the property portfolios and, as well as more single lets, we went on to invest in some HMOs as well. Some of the tenants who moved in back in 2011/2012 are still with us today.

Tax Breaks

When the Government starting talking about introducing something called Clause 24 (now Section 24) which removes the ability for property owners with mortgages in their own names to offset their mortgage interest against rent before tax is calculated, we started to look for a way to mitigate that tax. This was when we rediscovered Serviced Accommodation (SA) or short-term rentals. There are many tax advantages with this strategy, including the avoidance of Section 24 and an amazing tax saving through claiming Capital Allowances (CAs). CAs on SA properties allow you to earn tens of thousands of pounds per property, tax-free! Once I knew about this strategy, I started converting my own BTL properties to

SA, as well as buying property specifically to use as SA, and renting property of other landlords to use as SA which is called Rent to SA (R2SA). From 2012 onwards, I really wanted to spread the word about property investing and the opportunity it represents.

We ran a property networking event for three years in Swansea in order to be around like-minded people. I delivered property training events for Forces personnel as well as civilians and I also mentored people on property investing. It felt great being around people like me, who were all interested creating life-changing income from property.

The Lasting Effects of War

Remembrance Day for a long time has been an important date in my diary but making it the day I also left the army without the need to get a job, made it an even more emotional day. I first fully understood this on the first anniversary of me leaving the army. I was helping out as the MC at a property training event and I was asked to take control of the room for the two-minute silence and read Laurence Binyon's lines ("They shall not grow old ...") My voice was trembling as I spoke and my legs were visibly shaking underneath me. Due to the emotion I was feeling, it really affected the audience and many people were crying. I got off the stage and found a side room that had spare tables and chairs in and I wept uncontrollably for several minutes before regaining my composure. I do a lot of public speaking, quite often at weekends, but I now try to avoid speaking engagements on Remembrance Day if at all possible, although it is gradually getting easier for me as the years progress.

Something else that affects me significantly is the sound of a Chinook helicopter. I can be going about my daily business and the sound of those very distinctive rotor blades can turn me to stone. I guess it must take me back to times when I was feeling stress or fear such as the time we inserted into FOB Robinson.

Recent Years

Delivering Life Changing Property Investment Training

From 2017 to the current day, I have been delivering a Serviced Accommodation training course which Caroline and I wrote, to hundreds of people wanting to change their lives for the better. We have some amazing success stories of people we have trained that can be read about in my book *Serviced Accommodation Success* which was published in 2020 and was a number one best seller on Amazon. It is one of the most rewarding feelings I have experienced in my life, to hear that someone no longer has to worry about money, or they can now spend more time with their family – or both – due to the training they have received from us! I feel incredibly blessed to have found a career as a full-time property investor working for myself but also helping others be able to do the same too. I am a firm believer in leading by example and I will never ask someone to do something unless I have done it myself, but also only if I firmly believe it is in their best interest. This is so much nicer than the times in my army career when I had to ask people to put themselves in harm's way.

I still like to go back to Army reunions to meet up with old friends and I am glad that some of my friendships have really stood the test of time. There has been the odd occasion when an Army friend thinks I have become a bit big for my boots and have changed too much, but that's inevitable I suppose and I try not to lose any sleep over it.

29 Commando Reunion with my Dad Jock

I am finally in a happy, long-term relationship and my daughter Sian is doing fantastically well as a modern languages teacher at a very prestigious school. She is fluent in Spanish, French and German. Well done, Sian!

STOLL

A couple of years after I left the Army, I was contacted by a wonderful charity called STOLL who provide accommodation and training for homeless veterans, many of whom are suffering from PTSD. The charity initially asked me to give a talk to paying audience members about property investing and my transition from Army life in order to raise money. Since then, I have become involved in several fund-raising activities and even did one of the readings at their Christmas service at St Pauls in London in front of Royalty! Ok, not St Pauls Cathedral – it was St Pauls Church in Knightsbridge and not a well-known Royal, but I was very proud all the same!

Abseiling off the Broadgate Tower in aid of Stoll

Meeting Sophie Countess of Wessex

Vitality Charity Run Ending at Buckingham Palace

A fantastic event I attended was the opening of a new accommodation complex for the veterans called Centenary Lodge in Aldershot. I recorded a video of one of the veterans showing off his brand-new flat overlooking beautiful gardens which I have pinned on my Facebook page 'Property Soldier'.

As I stated at the beginning, 100% of the profits of this book will go to the charity and I urge you to visit their website stoll.org.uk to see the great work they do. If you would like to donate you can do so via my social media accounts.

Some of the Accommodation Provided by Stoll for Homeless Veterans

I want to thank you for buying this book and by doing so helping to raise money for homeless veterans. I urge you all to take stock of your life and decide whether you need to make changes. We need to make the most of this life we have been given: we owe it to ourselves and our friends and family to be happy. Often now, when I finish a social media post or a talk in front of a camera or from the stage, I point my finger at the audience – as per the Kitchener posters of WW1 – and say, "Remember: your future needs you!"

If you have found this book to be interesting or useful in any way, please share it on your social media as every purchase will raise money for homeless veterans.

Thank you for reading

Kevin Poneskis
Property Soldier
www.propertysoldier.co.uk

Printed in Great Britain
by Amazon